CORONAVIRUS:
THE COVID-19 PANDEMIC

BY SUE BRADFORD EDWARDS

CONTENT CONSULTANT

KRYS M. JOHNSON, PHD, MPH, CPH
ASSISTANT PROFESSOR, DEPARTMENT OF EPIDEMIOLOGY
AND BIOSTATISTICS
TEMPLE UNIVERSITY

Essential Library

An Imprint of Abdo Publishing | abdobooks.com

abdobooks.com

Published by Abdo Publishing, a division of ABDO, PO Box 398166, Minneapolis, Minnesota 55439. Copyright © 2021 by Abdo Consulting Group, Inc. International copyrights reserved in all countries. No part of this book may be reproduced in any form without written permission from the publisher. Essential Library™ is a trademark and logo of Abdo Publishing.

Printed in the United States of America, North Mankato, Minnesota.
072020
092020

Cover Photo: Kim Jong-un/Yonhap/AP Images,
Interior Photos: Darley Shen/Reuters/Newscom, 4–5; STR/AFP/Getty Images, 8; Dake Kang/AP Images, 12, 97; Ted S. Warren/AP Images, 14, 68; NIAID-RML/ Science Source, 16–17; Robert Nickelsberg/Getty Images News/Getty Images, 23; Shutterstock Images, 25; iStockphoto, 26–27, 38–39, 60–61; Kathy Willens/ AP Images, 29; Aijaz Rahi/AP Images, 30; Eyepix/Cover Images/AP Images, 35; Universal History Archive/Universal Images Group/Getty Images, 42; Nicolas McComber/iStockphoto, 44; Peter Hermes Furian/Shutterstock Images, 49; Krisztian Bocsi/Bloomberg/Getty Images, 50–51; Marco Garcia/AP Images, 54; John Minchillo/ AP Images, 58–59; Ulrich Perrey/picture-alliance/dpa/AP Images, 65; Buda Mendes/ Getty Images News/Getty Images, 72–73; Erin McGoff/iStockphoto, 74–75; Rogelio V. Solis/AP Images, 79; Mary Altaffer/AP Images, 82–83; John Moore/Getty Images News/Getty Images, 89; Chine Nouvelle/SIPA/Newscom, 92–93; Ahn Young-joon/AP Images, 95

Editor: Charly Haley
Series Designer: Maggie Villaume

Library of Congress Control Number: 2020935593

Publisher's Cataloging-in-Publication Data

Names: Edwards, Sue Bradford, author.
Title: Coronavirus: the COVID-19 pandemic / by Sue Bradford Edwards
Other title: the COVID-19 pandemic
Description: Minneapolis, Minnesota : Abdo Publishing, 2021 | Series: Special reports
       | Includes online resources and index
Identifiers: ISBN 9781532194009 (lib. bdg.) | ISBN 9781098212841 (ebook)
Subjects: LCSH: Epidemics--Juvenile literature. | Virus diseases--Juvenile literature.
       | Quarantine--Juvenile literature. | Interpersonal relations--Juvenile literature.
Classification: DDC 614.4--dc23

CONTENTS

Chapter One
WATCHING WUHAN 4

Chapter Two
CORONAVIRUSES 16

Chapter Three
THE SPREAD OF COVID-19 26

Chapter Four
PANDEMIC RESPONSES 38

Chapter Five
TESTING FOR COVID-19 50

Chapter Six
TREATING COVID-19 60

Chapter Seven
ECONOMIC IMPACT 74

Chapter Eight
RACIAL AND CULTURAL DISPARITIES 82

Chapter Nine
THE FUTURE 92

Essential Facts 100   Source Notes 106

Glossary 102   Index 110

Additional Resources 104   About the Author 112

WATCHING
WUHAN

On December 10, 2019, Wei Guixian, a vendor at the Huanan Seafood Wholesale Market, a live animal market in Wuhan, China, went to her local clinic. She thought she was getting a cold. The staff at the clinic treated her symptoms, and then she went back to work. Other vendors from this market also became sick with cold-like symptoms and visited a variety of clinics. When doctors at these different clinics realized that they were seeing a widespread illness—one that started out mild but then got more serious, sometimes becoming pneumonia—Wei and the other patients were quarantined. But Chinese government officials warned the doctors not to tell the public what was happening. They feared it might cause panic.

The Huanan Seafood Wholesale Market closed weeks after several market vendors began developing symptoms from an unknown virus.

PNEUMONIA

When a person has fluid in one or both lungs, doctors say he or she has pneumonia. The air sacs that make up the lungs fill with liquid, and this causes the person who has pneumonia to cough and feel short of breath. Because of the infection, the patient also runs a fever. Pneumonia can be caused by a virus (such as a coronavirus or influenza), a bacterium, or even a fungus. Pneumonia is not always serious, but if the infection is extreme enough, it can be life-threatening.

"I DON'T THINK HE WAS RUMOR-MONGERING. HASN'T THIS TURNED INTO REALITY NOW?"[2]

—LI SHUYING, FATHER OF DR. LI WENLIANG, 2020

Despite this warning, some doctors believed it was their responsibility to alert others about the seriousness of what they were seeing. On December 30, 2019, Dr. Li Wenliang messaged some of his medical school classmates in an online chat room. He told them that although he and other doctors did not know what virus was causing the pneumonia, the symptoms resembled those of severe acute respiratory syndrome (SARS). Four days later, China's Public Security Bureau forced Li to sign a document that said he had been warned to stop making "false comments."[1]

On December 31, 2019, Chinese health officials contacted the World Health Organization (WHO) to report this mysterious outbreak of viral pneumonia. At this point, dozens of patients had been hospitalized in the city of

Wuhan, which is in Hubei Province in central China. Before being hospitalized, the people had fevers, coughed, and had trouble breathing. Chest X-rays showed masses in their lungs that indicated they had pneumonia.

Many of those infected had worked in or visited the Huanan Seafood Wholesale Market. Because of this, medical officials suspected the illness might have come from one or more of the animals sold at the market. Vendors sold live sea animals, snakes, and bats. On January 1, 2020, the market was closed for a thorough cleaning to kill any possible germs. But doctors still did not know what was causing the illness.

By January 2, 2020, officials had collected a variety of data on the patients. One group of patients was a family. Early symptoms of the illness included fever, coughing,

LI WENLIANG

Dr. Li posted on the Chinese blogging site Weibo that he started coughing on January 10, 2020. The next day, he began running a fever, and two days later he was hospitalized. It wasn't until January 30 that he was diagnosed with the mysterious illness, which by then had been named COVID-19. On February 7, 2020, Li died from the disease. He was 34 years old. News of his death gained a lot of attention on Chinese social media, with comments calling for an apology by the government and an investigation into this death.

and fatigue, with patients sometimes producing mucus, experiencing headaches, or having diarrhea.

Officials found that the first known patient to show symptoms had gotten sick on December 1, 2019, much earlier than had originally been reported. No one related

As more and more people were found to have the mysterious viral illness, hospitals in Wuhan became overwhelmed by the need for treatment.

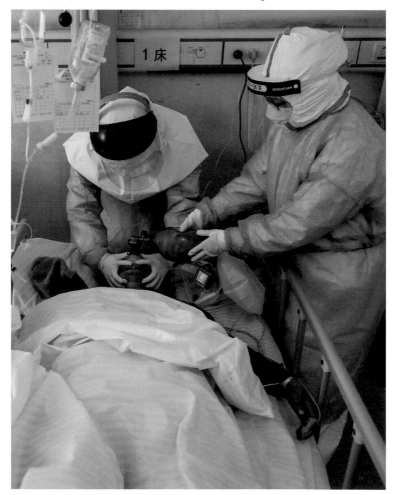

to this patient showed symptoms, and this patient could not be linked in any way to the later patients, including those connected to the market. This meant that the market may not have been the source and that the illness, still unidentified, was probably more widespread than officials had previously thought.

By January 5, 2020, the patients had been screened to determine what virus had caused the pneumonia. Through this screening, health officials ruled out SARS, Middle East respiratory syndrome (MERS), influenza, and even adenoviruses, a family of viruses that cause fever, sore throats, pink eye, and pneumonia. By January 6, there were 59 known patients suffering from the unidentified illness.[3]

On January 9, 2020, the WHO reported that Chinese authorities had discovered that one of the patients had been infected by a novel, or new, coronavirus. It didn't take long for officials to realize that this virus, severe acute respiratory syndrome coronavirus 2 (SARS-CoV-2), had caused the illness that led to the mysterious cases of pneumonia. The WHO named the new illness coronavirus disease 2019 (COVID-19).

MORE TO THE
STORY

ZOONOTIC DISEASES

Any illness that can be passed from animals to humans is known as a zoonotic disease. Because coronaviruses are known to be zoonotic, authorities initially thought that people caught COVID-19 from animals at the Wuhan market. Zoonotic diseases can be transmitted in many different ways. When a tick carrying the bacteria that cause Lyme disease bites someone, the bacteria can be passed to this person. When someone eats undercooked or contaminated food from animals, such as chicken, they can get food poisoning caused by the salmonella bacteria. People can also get these bacteria by handling live birds or reptiles. The fungal infection that causes ringworm comes from cattle. People can limit the risk of catching a zoonotic disease by avoiding animal bites or scratches, keeping their faces away from animals in petting zoos, and washing their hands after being around animals. Authorities have since realized the Wuhan market may not have been the source of COVID-19, but scientists have continued researching which animals may have passed the novel coronavirus to humans.

EPIDEMIC OR PANDEMIC?

Governments and scientists around the world began to monitor the situation, trying to judge whether COVID-19 would remain an epidemic or become a pandemic. According to the US Centers for Disease Control and Prevention (CDC), an epidemic is characterized by a sudden increase beyond what is normal in the number of people who have a disease or illness. An epidemic might infect people in one city, country, or continent.

A pandemic is when an illness has spread around the world, spreads from one person to another, and has caused a large number of people to become sick or die. In 2009, a strain of H1N1 influenza known as swine flu caused a pandemic that was first detected in the

SWINE FLU PANDEMIC

In 2009, a strain of H1N1 influenza virus mutated, or changed, into something highly infectious and spread rapidly through populations around the world. Part of the problem was that this virus, which came to be called the swine flu because it was genetically similar to influenza viruses found in swine or pigs, was different from other H1N1 viruses that were active at that time. Because of this, it was not covered by seasonal flu vaccinations. It was similar to an older strain of the H1N1, a strain that many people older than age 60 had been exposed to. Because these older people had fought it off before, they had antibodies which may have helped them in 2009, whereas many young people, who had not been previously exposed, became ill.

United States, eventually killing up to 575,400 worldwide in a single year.[4]

Scientists and government officials know that early action can limit the number of illnesses and deaths in a pandemic. Because of this, Taiwan, a small island only 81 miles (130 km) from China, took an especially aggressive approach toward the coronavirus. On December 31, 2019, officials from the Taiwan Centers for Disease Control started meeting planes as they landed, boarding to check each passenger for symptoms. As the situation in China worsened, the Taiwanese government reached out to everyone who had traveled to Taiwan from Wuhan since

A Wuhan airport staff member checks travelers' temperatures in January 2020.

December 20. These people were closely monitored to see whether they developed symptoms like the patients in Wuhan.

By this time, officials from other countries around the world that were connected with Wuhan by air travel were on high alert. Health officials screened all travelers coming from the city. They looked for unexplained symptoms that could be related to COVID-19.

A group of scientists worked to sequence the genetic material in the virus. By January 10, this code had been posted online at GenBank, the genetic-sequence database maintained by the National Center for Biotechnology Information in the United States. As part of an international collaboration of genetic databases, the information at GenBank is available to scientists worldwide. Once the genetic sequence was online, scientists could begin work to find treatments and perhaps a vaccine.

One of these scientists was David Ho, who developed a treatment for acquired immunodeficiency syndrome (AIDS). AIDS is a disease that damages the immune system, leaving those who suffer from it more likely to develop infections and certain cancers. In studying AIDS, Ho discovered that drugs known as protease inhibitors kept the virus from being able to duplicate itself and make the patient sick. Ho wanted to try to develop a similar treatment for COVID-19. Another researcher who had been monitoring the situation was Olfert Landt, a German scientist who had developed tests to diagnose other

A patient is loaded into an ambulance outside of a nursing home in Kirkland, Washington, the site of one of the United States' first COVID-19 outbreaks.

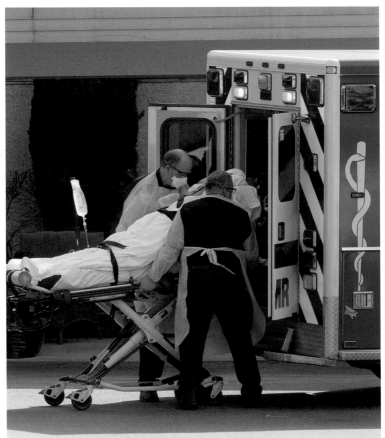

coronavirus infections. With the seriousness of COVID-19 and the rapid spread of infection, scientists believed a pandemic was likely.

On January 19, 2020, a 35-year-old man visited a clinic in Snohomish County in Washington State. He had been running a fever and coughing for four days. He was given a face mask and put it on before taking a seat in the waiting room, where he remained for 20 minutes. Then he was taken to an exam room, where he told staff that on January 15 he had returned to the United States after visiting family in Wuhan, China. With this patient in Washington, it became clear the novel coronavirus was in the United States.

By January 24, 2020, there were at least 870 COVID-19 cases in China, and 26 of these patients had died. The illness had spread beyond the city of Wuhan and the province of Hubei to 25 Chinese provinces. There were 19 more confirmed cases of COVID-19 across ten other countries around the world.[5] Doctors and governments had to protect people from this new, fast-moving illness. But there was still much to learn about the novel coronavirus.

CHAPTER TWO

CORONAVIRUSES

A virus is a microscopic particle. Like many bacteria and fungi, viruses cause disease. Scientists are still learning about viruses, and there is no clear consensus on whether viruses should be considered living or nonliving. A virus depends on a living host, such as a person it has infected. But a virus contains some of the basic building blocks of all living organisms. At its center is a mass of nucleic acid carrying genetic code, either deoxyribonucleic acid (DNA) or ribonucleic acid (RNA). Viruses have a unique structure around these nucleic acids, a protein layer called the capsid. Some viruses, including coronaviruses, have another layer called the envelope.

Viruses are able to duplicate themselves. To do this, the virus enters the body of a host. Once the virus is inside a host's body, it attaches itself to the outside

The novel coronavirus, SARS-CoV-2, shown through an electron microscope

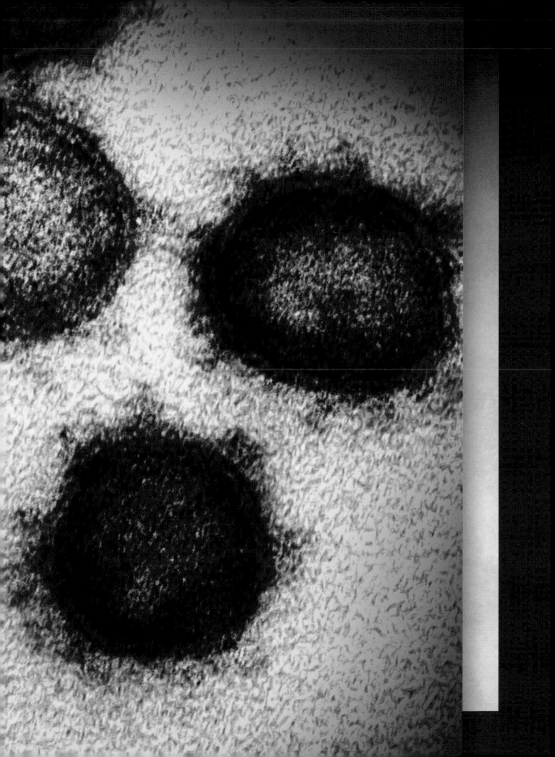

of one of the host's cells. Every cell is surrounded by a cell membrane, and the virus punctures this membrane and then injects its DNA or RNA into the host cell, infecting it. The cell is taken over by the virus and used to make more virus cells. The virus continues to infect more cells within the host. When this happens, the host is contagious and can spread the infection, whether the host is an animal infecting a human or one human infecting another.

THE CORONAVIRUS FAMILY

Coronaviruses are a large family of viruses that feature an envelope covered in spike proteins. Because of these proteins, researchers initially thought coronaviruses looked as if they were surrounded by a halo of spikes like the spikes on a crown, which is how the viruses got their name. *Corona* is the Latin word for crown.

Coronaviruses can infect a variety of animals, including camels, bats, and birds. Some evidence points to bats as being the original animal host to SARS-CoV-2. When a virus moves from one population to another, including from an animal population to the human population, this is known as a spillover. Sometimes this happens because the virus has mutated, or changed, and can for the first time infect people. Other times it is because people are coming into contact with the animal hosts more often than before and thus have a greater chance of contracting the virus. This can happen when people expand a city, building in a new area that is also the host animal's habitat.

Different coronaviruses cause different diseases. Some cause gastrointestinal illnesses with stomach cramps, nausea, and diarrhea. Others lead to mild

RNA

RNA is the genetic material found in SARS-CoV-2. RNA forms single strands made up of four types of molecules known as bases: adenine, guanine, cytosine, and uracil. This strand doesn't lie flat but forms a helix, or spiral. Coronaviruses have especially long RNA strands, ranging from 26,000 to 32,000 bases in length. The protein that coronaviruses use to replicate these genetic chains is called RNA-dependent RNA polymerase. This protein is prone to mistakes when replicating RNA, leading to changes in the sequence of bases. These changes are mutations. SARS-CoV-2 may have infected humans because of such mutations.

respiratory illnesses, causing colds. Two coronaviruses that almost always lead to serious respiratory illness are the SARS and MERS viruses, which have both been compared to SARS-CoV-2.

The SARS virus was first found in China in 2003. Its animal host was the civet, which looks similar to a cat. Eventually SARS spread to 8,000 people in 29 countries. Approximately 800 people died.[1] In SARS, the first symptom is a high fever. This leads to a headache and body aches. SARS was found to spread through close contact with other people.

The MERS virus was first identified in Saudi Arabia in 2012. It spread to humans from camels. MERS symptoms start with a fever and include shortness of breath and a cough. The disease killed three to four out of every ten people who got sick. All cases were linked to the Arabian Peninsula. A 2015 outbreak in South Korea was traced to a person who had traveled to Saudi Arabia and then back to South Korea.

THE NOVEL CORONAVIRUS

A novel virus is a virus that has never before been sampled or studied. The novel coronavirus that causes COVID-19 was first seen in Wuhan.

Not everyone infected with SARS-CoV-2 knows they are sick. Some infected people may have no symptoms at all, but they can still pass the virus to others. The most common symptoms are fever, dry cough, and trouble breathing. Other symptoms include sore throat, aches and pains, exhaustion, headache, vomiting, diarrhea, and loss of sense of taste or smell.

"THE SEEMINGLY SIMPLE QUESTION OF WHETHER OR NOT VIRUSES ARE ALIVE, WHICH MY STUDENTS OFTEN ASK, HAS PROBABLY DEFIED A SIMPLE ANSWER ALL THESE YEARS BECAUSE IT RAISES A FUNDAMENTAL ISSUE: WHAT EXACTLY DEFINES 'LIFE?'"[2]

—LUIS VILLARREAL, DIRECTOR OF THE CENTER FOR VIRUS RESEARCH, UNIVERSITY OF CALIFORNIA, IRVINE

Some COVID-19 patients become severely ill; their breathing problems worsen to the point where they are not getting enough oxygen. They need to be hospitalized. A patient may be given oxygen through a breathing mask or a nasal cannula, a lightweight tube that delivers oxygen into a patient's nostrils. In the most severe situations, a person may be put on a ventilator, a machine that feeds oxygen into the lungs through a tube inserted in the mouth, the nose, or a hole surgically cut into the neck.

In serious cases, the virus also attacks internal organs. It invades the bloodstream and makes its way to organs such as the liver, heart, and kidneys. In these organs, the virus causes inflammation, which consists of swelling, irritation, and pain. This can cause permanent damage and is especially serious if a patient already has a medical condition involving one of these organs. This means that people who are at higher risk of dying from COVID-19 include people with kidney, heart, or liver disease, along with people who have asthma or diabetes. Other high-risk COVID-19 patients include elderly people, people who are severely obese, and people with compromised immune systems.

But not all serious cases of COVID-19 involve patients who have these preexisting conditions. As the pandemic unfolded, scientists were still learning about what contributed to various cases. "We had a young woman in

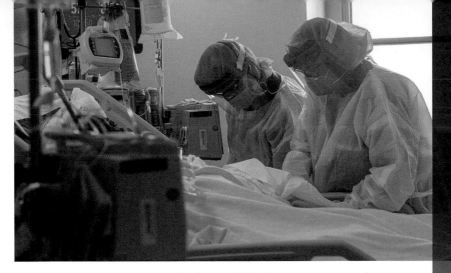

Nurses check on a COVID-19 patient on a ventilator in the intensive care unit of a New York City hospital.

her early 30s who came in with a profound stroke, the kind of stroke that leaves someone permanently paralyzed and possibly unable to survive," said Dr. J. Mocco of the Mount Sinai Health System in New York.[3] The stroke was caused by a blood clot that limited blood flow to the woman's brain. Because she had no risk factors for a stroke, doctors tested her for a range of issues and found COVID-19.

Doctors around the world saw COVID-19 patients with this clotting disorder. Some had tiny clots in their lungs. Others had clots in their legs or kidneys. Because the virus causes a respiratory illness, doctors worked to figure out why it was causing blood clots. This was just one aspect of the disease that scientists and doctors were studying in mid-2020. The novel coronavirus had no cure and no vaccine, and it was infecting people all around the world.

FROM THE HEADLINES

HOW TO BATTLE A VIRUS

Early in the coronavirus pandemic, people bought every cleaning product they thought would kill the virus. Stores found it difficult to keep hand sanitizers, wipes, and bleach on their shelves, although some experts say bleach, while effective, is unnecessary against coronavirus. Using bleach to kill SARS-CoV-2 is like using a bludgeon instead of a flyswatter to kill a fly, according to virologist Jane Greatorex from Cambridge University in the United Kingdom.

All viruses are bundles of genetic code that travel around inside proteins and lipids, or fatty acids. Some viruses, including SARS-CoV-2, are wrapped in a fat-based casing. Although these casings mean that viruses can survive for hours at a time on the ground or on hard surfaces such as door handles or cardboard boxes, the good news is that this casing can be destroyed with soap. Once this happens, the bits of genetic code are washed away. Because the coronavirus cannot enter the body through the skin on a person's hand, handwashing is enough to destroy the virus and avoid infection.

Stores struggled to keep cleaning products in stock as customers panicked about the emerging pandemic.

CHAPTER THREE

THE SPREAD OF
COVID-19

B y January 20, 2020, the first cases of COVID-19 outside of China had been reported in Japan, South Korea, and Thailand. The disease quickly spread to other parts of the world. On February 2, the first death outside of China was reported in the Philippines when a traveler from Wuhan died. The first death in Europe happened on February 14 when a Chinese tourist died in Paris, France.

On February 19, the first two cases in Iran were announced. Both people later died.[1] On February 26, Brazil announced the first case in Latin America, a businessman from São Paulo who had just returned from a trip to Italy. Three days later, on February 29, the United States reported what officials believed was the

International travel allowed COVID-19 to spread to different countries around the world.

first coronavirus death in the country, although officials later realized two other people had died earlier from the virus.[2]

There are several ways the novel coronavirus spread to create the COVID-19 pandemic. The virus spread around the world quickly through air travel, leading many countries to eventually issue travel bans in an attempt to curb the pandemic. Within communities, the virus spread from person to person and was highly contagious.

TRAVEL BANS

Travel bans began with the Chinese government's January 23 ban on travel to and from Wuhan. Train stations and other transportation systems in the city were shut down. Not long afterwards, the United States issued its own ban. On January 31, the US government blocked travel into the country by nonresidents who had traveled to China. On March 11, the government expanded the ban to include those who had visited Iran and a group of European countries. On March 21, it closed the Mexican and Canadian borders to travelers. However, trade shipments were still allowed to pass through, and US

As a result of travel bans, normally busy airports became nearly empty.

citizens who had been abroad could return home through

designated airports where their health would be checked.

Wanting to learn how travel bans altered the spread of

the virus, a group of public health and computer-modeling

scientists from around the world created a program to

represent the virus's spread. Their model showed that

the Wuhan travel ban delayed the spread of the virus

throughout the rest of China by three to five days. The

model also revealed that the ban reduced the spread of

the virus to other parts of the world by 77 percent but that

this reduction lasted for only two to three weeks.[3] This

computer model demonstrated that restricting travel from

China had a long-term impact only when combined with global efforts to prevent person-to-person spread, such as asking people to stay home as much as possible to avoid infecting one another.

Travel bans only slow the spread of the virus by preventing additional infected people from entering a region. They don't stop the spread of the virus in regions where it is already present. This is what happened in the United States. The US government did not issue a travel ban until after the man in Snohomish County, Washington, was found to have COVID-19. He had had a fever and cough for four days before he saw a CDC

When people had to travel during the pandemic, they often wore face masks to avoid spreading the virus.

bulletin about the coronavirus outbreak in Wuhan and went to a clinic. Although he had not visited the seafood market or knowingly been in contact with anyone who was sick with COVID-19, on January 20 his test results came back positive, and he was admitted to the hospital for observation as the first American COVID-19 patient. On March 11, 2020, the WHO declared COVID-19 a pandemic. This was also the day that the United States banned foreign travelers who had visited China, Iran, and some European countries within the previous two weeks. By that point, the virus had already been in the United States for almost two months.

PERSON TO PERSON

Within a country or community, COVID-19 spreads through respiratory droplets during close personal contact. When people sneeze, cough, or speak, these droplets of saliva are propelled into the air. Many of these droplets—and any virus they may contain—land on the ground. Other droplets remain in the air and may enter another person's mouth, nose, or eyes. This is why health experts asked

MASKS

Because of how COVID-19 spreads from person to person, many people wore face masks to reduce the spread. The CDC recommended that members of the general public not wear medical masks and N95 masks, also known as respirators, because these were needed by medical professionals. Instead, on April 3, 2020, the organization recommended that people wear other face coverings, such as homemade cloth masks, any time they went somewhere they could not properly distance themselves from others. This included wearing masks when going to the grocery store or the pharmacy. One reason the CDC made this recommendation was that infected people who did not have symptoms could still spread the virus.

people to keep a distance from each other during the pandemic.

Still, other droplets end up on the sick person's hand when he or she covers a cough or a sneeze and can be spread with a handshake or other direct contact. If an uninfected person gets the virus on his hand and touches his nose or mouth, he can infect himself. This is why handwashing is important in reducing the spread of COVID-19. Because infected people may not look sick, they can spread COVID-19 to friends and neighbors without anyone realizing it.

When studying the spread of a disease, one key measure is known as the basic reproduction number, or $R0$ (pronounced "r-naught"). The $R0$ is the average number of people infected by each sick individual. For example, the $R0$ for most strains of influenza is 1.5. If a disease's $R0$

is lower than 1, the disease will decline and eventually fade away. If it is 1, the number of infections will remain at the same level. And if it is higher than 1, the number of infections will increase. The higher the R0 is, the harder the disease will be to control. Researchers at the Abdul Latif Jameel Institute for Disease and Emergency Analytics in London calculated the R0 for SARS-CoV-2 to be about 2.9.

"A SNEEZING OR COUGHING PERSON WILL COVER THEIR MOUTH, GET IT ALL OVER THEIR HAND, AND THEN TOUCH SOMETHING THAT YOU THEN TOUCH."[5]

—DR. ROBERT MURPHY, INFECTIOUS DISEASE EXPERT, NORTHWESTERN UNIVERSITY, 2020

Researchers at the Los Alamos National Laboratory in New Mexico found that when they looked at data from Wuhan, the R0 was 2.2 to 2.7, but when they used data from across China, the number jumped to 5.7.[4] An R0 varies based on population, crowding, and other factors. Scientists continued working to determine the R0 for SARS-CoV-2.

MISSED OPPORTUNITIES

Officials can only effectively limit the spread of a virus when they know where it is. In late January 2020, Dr. Helen Chu, an infectious disease specialist with the

MORE TO THE
STORY

SUPER SPREADERS

A super spreader is a person or group who infects a much larger number of people than average. Super spreaders accelerate the circulation of the virus. In South Korea, one woman known as Patient 31 infected at least 37 people at the Shincheonji Church of Jesus in the city of Daegu.[6] After developing a fever, she decided not to be tested because she had not traveled outside the country. Then she attended four separate church services before being diagnosed in February.

On March 5, 2020, a man from Johannesburg, South Africa, attended a birthday party for a friend in Westport, Connecticut. After the party, he flew home and started showing symptoms on the airplane. By that point he had already exposed all 50 party guests to the virus. More than half of the party guests were later diagnosed, but not before they returned to their homes across the United States.[7]

University of Washington, was part of a research program studying the distribution of influenza in the Puget Sound region of coastal Washington State. She read a medical journal article about the COVID-19 patient in Snohomish County and knew the region had only a limited time to prepare, but her team could help officials discover how widespread the virus already was. In studying influenza, they had been collecting nasal swabs like those used to test for COVID-19.

One COVID-19 test involves a medical professional using a nasal swab to get a sample from a patient.

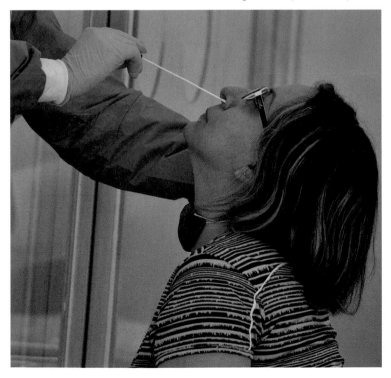

But to run the COVID-19 test on the specimens they had collected, Chu's team needed federal and state permission to avoid breaking the law. The people who had offered samples for Chu's study had signed waivers that gave the researchers permission to look for influenza, but additional permission would be required to look for the novel coronavirus. In addition, the lab in which Chu worked was certified for research but not to make medical diagnoses. Chu contacted the appropriate federal and state officials but was denied permission to perform the COVID-19 test.

By February 25, Chu had discussed the situation with her team, and they all agreed that even without government permission, they needed to test for COVID-19. A month had gone by, and they believed their research might be the only way for Seattle to avoid a dangerous outbreak like

TESTING DELAY

In April 2018, the CDC and three lab testing associations came up with a plan on how to respond quickly in a public health crisis. The plan involved increasing the capacity of public health labs and also utilizing private labs to coordinate the large-scale response needed to contain the spread of an outbreak and save lives. In 2020, the US Department of Health and Human Services blocked these temporary measures. It did this due to regulations designed to protect patient privacy and health. This delay dealt a sharp blow to testing capabilities.

the one that had occurred in Wuhan. The researchers ran the coronavirus test and found a teenage boy infected with the virus. He had not traveled to China or anywhere else. This meant that COVID-19 was spreading in the Puget Sound region, and no one had known.

After Chu's team realized the teen had the coronavirus, health officials began to look for COVID-19 and discovered that two people had already died of the virus. Twenty more people in the region would soon die of COVID-19. On March 4, 2020, a review board gave Chu's team permission to report its COVID-19 test results to the infected participants and health authorities. But with the delays in testing, Seattle became the first hot spot in the United States for COVID-19. By June 1, King County, which includes Seattle, had 8,161 cases with 569 dead. Seattle was the first, but soon there were other US hot spots. These included Cook County, Illinois, where Chicago is located—with 77,925 cases and 3,642 dead by June 1— and New York City, with 208,085 cases and 21,050 dead by this same date.[8]

CHAPTER FOUR

PANDEMIC
RESPONSES

Governments and medical experts around the world used many strategies to address the COVID-19 pandemic. Because COVID-19 spreads mainly from person to person, quarantining and distancing became primary ways to keep people healthy because they keep people away from one another. Some strategies worked better than others. People were still learning about the virus as it spread.

In addressing COVID-19, medical and government experts, as well as the public, looked to past pandemics to try to understand what was coming. COVID-19 is often compared to SARS. But SARS was largely wiped out in about a year, something that experts warned would be impossible with COVID-19.[1] People with

Many people quarantined themselves in their homes and only saw others at a distance during the pandemic.

SARS had symptoms for several days before they became contagious, while COVID-19 is often contagious before symptoms appear. Because SARS symptoms are visible before the infection is contagious, patients can be quarantined early and the spread of the virus can be interrupted. This is more difficult to do with COVID-19 because infected people can spread the virus before showing symptoms or without ever showing symptoms.

EBOLA

Some people compare COVID-19 to Ebola, a virus that causes fever and internal bleeding, or hemorrhaging. Hemorrhaging is a frightening symptom, and about 50 percent of people who contract Ebola die.[2] This is probably why people think of Ebola when pandemics are mentioned. But Ebola was a West African epidemic, not a pandemic, because it never spread in communities worldwide. Ebola is not very contagious. It has a reproduction number of 1.5 to 2. This is low in part because Ebola is spread through bodily fluids such as blood or vomit, which can be easily avoided.

INFLUENZA OUTBREAK

Possibly the closest pandemic comparison to COVID-19 is the influenza outbreak of 1918–1919. People called it the Spanish flu, though experts do not know where the disease originated. The virus infected approximately 500 million people, or one-third of the planet's population. It killed at least 50 million people worldwide, with approximately 675,000 of these deaths in the United States.[3] Anyone can be infected by influenza, but it is usually only life-threatening for certain groups of people, including children younger than two years, people older than 65 years, pregnant women, or anyone with asthma, diabetes, or a heart problem. The 1918 flu was a unique influenza strain because many of the dead were otherwise healthy people from 20 to 40 years old. The death rate varied from place to place based on the approach taken by local authorities.

Philadelphia, Pennsylvania, and Saint Louis, Missouri, were among the ten largest US cities at the time of the influenza outbreak. Philadelphia officials didn't want to disrupt daily life. They went ahead with a parade to promote the war bonds that helped fund World War I (1914–1918). The parade was a success, drawing hundreds of thousands of spectators—and the virus spread. The flu ended up killing 20,000 people in Philadelphia.[4] Saint Louis took the opposite approach. Like Philadelphia's leaders, Saint Louis's mayor was reluctant to take drastic actions. But he did follow health officials' recommendations and closed gathering places, including schools, churches,

A Seattle streetcar driver denies entrance to a man not wearing a mask during the flu pandemic in 1918.

sporting events, and bars. In the end, Saint Louis saw a much lower death toll, with 2,910 people killed in the 1918 flu pandemic.[5]

SOCIAL DISTANCING

As Saint Louis did during the influenza outbreak, many communities implemented social distancing measures during the COVID-19 pandemic. Social distancing, also called physical distancing, is the idea that when outside of their homes, people should stay a minimum of six feet (1.8 m) apart. That way, even if someone who is sick sneezes or coughs, the distance will reduce the chance that the virus can spread to those around them. People were instructed to avoid gathering in groups, which limited the operation of schools, restaurants, and more.

The US government first developed a plan for social distancing in 2005 when President George W. Bush contacted scientists and asked them how Americans could survive a hypothetical bioterrorist attack that involved a virus. By February 2007, a CDC plan for slowing a pandemic called Non-Pharmaceutical Interventions (NPIs) became the official US policy. Among other strategies, the plan included social distancing. The plan was updated in April 2017 under President Barack Obama.

President Donald Trump eventually used these plans to address the COVID-19 pandemic. Initially, Trump downplayed the seriousness of the virus. "It's going to disappear. One day, it's like a miracle, it will disappear," Trump said on February 28, 2020.[6] But on March 16, Trump asked that for 15 days, Americans avoid travel and not gather in groups larger than ten people. On March 26, 2020, the United States became the country with the most COVID-19 cases in the world, with 83,836 confirmed cases.[7]

Some stores limited the number of people
inside to help customers keep their distance from each other.
People distanced while waiting in line outside as well.

Days later, the Trump administration's social distancing recommendation was extended through the end of April. On April 7, a count by Johns Hopkins University in Baltimore, Maryland, showed the United States had more than 2,000 COVID-19 deaths in one day, surpassing the nation's usual leading cause of death, heart disease, which kills approximately 1,772 people per day.[8]

Governors across the United States issued statewide policies to reduce the spread of COVID-19. On March 19, 2020, California governor Gavin Newsom ordered all residents to shelter in place. This order asked people to only leave their homes for necessary trips, such as to buy food, and many businesses temporarily closed. Many other states followed suit with similar policies. In early May, Newsom announced that the state would reopen in phases starting with reopening some retail stores. Other states began slowly reopening around that time as well.

In addition to social distancing, many communities encouraged or required the quarantining of people with COVID-19. This was done in Vo, Italy. As the virus moved across Italy, Vo tested its entire population, even those with no symptoms. Of 3,300 people, 66 tested positive for the virus.[9] Most of these showed no symptoms. These people were quarantined in their homes for two weeks. Unlike most of Italy, which was seeing increasing numbers of COVID-19 patients, Vo's rate of infection dropped. Isolation and quarantine could slow the spread of the virus.

HERD IMMUNITY

Not every government was willing to put restrictions on citizens amid the pandemic. Some encouraged people to live as they normally would. The idea behind this approach was that though people would get sick in increasing numbers, the population would eventually develop herd immunity. This means once enough people have recovered from the virus and are therefore immune, the virus has too few people left to infect, and it gradually fades out.

A population develops herd immunity in two ways—by vaccination or by allowing the virus to spread naturally through the population. A vaccine was not available as COVID-19 spread around the world. Immunity by allowing the virus to spread naturally relies on antibodies. When someone is infected, the body produces antibodies to fight off the virus. If someone has antibodies and is once again infected by the same virus, the body might be able to fight off the infection early and prevent that person from getting sick.

"WE HAVE NOT YET ESTABLISHED THAT THOSE WHO RECOVER FROM THIS INFECTION INDEED DEVELOP LONG-TERM IMMUNITY. HERD IMMUNITY PROJECTIONS DEPEND COMPLETELY ON SUCH A SUSTAINED IMMUNE RESPONSE, AND WE HAVEN'T FOUND OUT WHETHER THAT EVEN EXISTS."[11]

—DR. GRETA BAUER, PROFESSOR OF EPIDEMIOLOGY AND BIOSTATISTICS AT WESTERN UNIVERSITY, ONTARIO, CANADA, 2020

To reach herd immunity, 70 to 90 percent of the population must recover from the infection and carry the antibodies.[10] However, as the COVID-19 pandemic unfolded, scientists did not yet know whether recovered victims produced enough antibody proteins to protect themselves from becoming sick again in the long term.

Sweden is one of the countries that attempted to build herd immunity by letting the virus move through its population. With COVID-19, this meant risking a large number of deaths, and more than 4,500 Swedish people died by June 3. The neighboring country of Finland, which has about one-half of Sweden's population, employed strict lockdowns, and its COVID-19 death toll was far lower, with 321 deaths.[12] Dr. Anders Tegnell, chief epidemiologist at Sweden's Public Health Agency, said too many Swedish people had died following the herd immunity strategy.

Initially the United Kingdom's government had planned to develop herd immunity. Then on March 16, 2020, the Imperial College London's COVID-19 Response Team released an estimate suggesting that 500,000 people in the United Kingdom would die before herd immunity developed.[13] On that day, the government changed its stance, telling people to practice social distancing and work from home. Two days later, all UK schools closed.

UK PRIME MINISTER BORIS JOHNSON

On April 5, 2020, news reporters announced that UK prime minister Boris Johnson, diagnosed with COVID-19, had been admitted to St. Thomas' Hospital in London. He had been running a high fever for more than ten days. Although his hospital stay was considered precautionary and not an emergency, he spent three days in the hospital's intensive care unit. The UK first secretary of state Dominic Raab ran the government until Johnson returned to duty on April 27, 2020.

FLATTENING THE CURVE

The reason most health-care experts encourage social distancing is to flatten the curve. The term *curve* refers to a graph of how many people get COVID-19 over a period of time. At first, there are only a small number of people with the virus, but as new people are infected and infect other people, the numbers rise. The curve of the graph gets steeper. As people recover from the infection or die, the number of infections peaks and then begins to drop.

Flattening the curve doesn't reduce the total number of people who get sick. Instead, it lowers the peak by stretching out the amount of infections over a longer period of time. This means that at the new peak, fewer people will be sick. Flattening the curve

TAIWAN

When Taiwan's government saw the dangers posed by COVID-19, it quickly began implementing a wide variety of protocols. Some rules restricted movement, including a policy that enabled the government to monitor the location of quarantined individuals using government-issued cell phones. Other regulations ensured that people would have access to protective gear. On January 30, 2020, mask prices were fixed at 27 cents each to keep sellers from raising prices for their own profit. On February 1, the price per mask was dropped to 20 cents. On February 3, Taiwan limited the number of masks each person could buy per week to two. These and other rules flattened the curve in Taiwan.[14]

The Curve

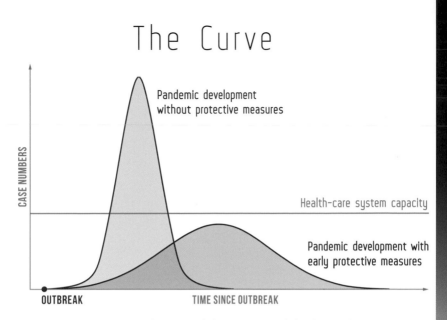

CASE NUMBERS

Pandemic development
without protective measures

Health-care system capacity

Pandemic development with
early protective measures

OUTBREAK   TIME SINCE OUTBREAK

Protective measures such as social distancing can help flatten the curve
of a pandemic so health-care systems do not become overwhelmed by high
numbers of patients needing care all at once.

prevents high numbers of sick people from overwhelming
health-care systems. As people become seriously ill,
they seek medical care and some are admitted into the
hospital. Because there are only so many doctors, nurses,
and hospital beds, only a limited number of people can
be treated at one time. When the peak number of sick
people surpasses what the health-care system can handle,
people die, unable to access health care. When the curve is
flattened, more people can be treated because they seek
medical help over a longer period of time. A pandemic
might last longer when the curve is flattened, but more
lives are saved.

CHAPTER FIVE

TESTING FOR
COVID-19

After New Year's Day 2020, German scientist Olfert Landt saw news reports about the novel coronavirus in China. He had developed tests for SARS, swine flu, and other viruses, and he suspected he could develop a test for this new virus as well. He read a lot and talked to virologists at a hospital in Berlin, Germany. By January 10, 2020, he had a workable test kit. In two months, his company, TIB Molbiol Syntheselabor GmbH, made 40,000 test kits, enough to test approximately four million people. Orders for the kits came in from the WHO and 60 different countries.[1]

The TIB tests use polymerase chain reaction, a diagnostic method that the WHO recommends. When labs get the test kit, they run a test using an engineered

Olfert Landt holds COVID-19 tests produced by his company. Each test kit includes 100 tests.

piece of virus. When this test comes back positive, the lab knows its equipment and the chemicals in the kit are working correctly. When patient swabs come in, a technician uses a substance called primer from the test kit to amplify the virus's genetic code. This means that even if the patient is showing no symptoms, the small amount of virus will still be detected. It only takes a few hours to receive test results.

The TIB test was not the only COVID-19 test developed. While many of the earliest COVID-19 tests were polymerase chain reaction tests, later blood tests looked for SARS-CoV-2 antibodies. While these tests can detect antibodies in a person's blood, they cannot reveal how long the person will have the antibodies. Some tests also cannot show whether someone currently has COVID-19, only that a person has recovered from the disease and has produced antibodies.

MAKING TEST KITS

Landt and his company worked hard to meet the high demand for COVID-19 test kits. TIB ran the machinery used to make the test kits day and night, seven days a week. The company needed extra help packaging and shipping the test kits, so Landt brought on a team of students who sat at long tables packing kits into plastic bags. Landt also purchased a machine just to fold the instructions so that they could fit into the bags. His son was in charge of labeling, a job that was supposed to be part time but ended up filling 60 hours a week.[2]

ADMINISTERING THE TESTS

Once these tests were developed, the medical community had to find a way to administer the tests to people who could be highly infectious without putting other patients or medical staff at risk. One way to minimize contact was to use drive-through test centers. These popped up in countries around the world, including South Korea, France, and the United States. Medical personnel wore protective clothing such as scrubs, masks, face shields, and gloves. Patients drove up and, while still in their cars, had their temperatures taken, had their hearts and lungs checked with a stethoscope, and answered questions. If the person qualified for a COVID-19 test based on symptoms, a long swab was inserted into the nostril to take a mucus sample high in the nasal cavity. The goal of these test sites was to keep people who may be infected away from doctor's offices, emergency rooms, or clinics where they could infect someone else.

As COVID-19 spread rapidly, a large number of governments and health agencies competed for the limited number of available test kits. In the United States,

Drive-through test sites limited the exposure of people who thought they might have COVID-19.

part of the problem was the length of time it takes to get a new test approved by the Food and Drug Administration (FDA). "This virus is faster than the FDA," said Dr. Alex Greninger, an assistant professor at the University of Washington Medical Center in Seattle, as he sought approval for a new test.[3] The FDA denied that it was slow to move forward and pointed out that within 24 hours of receiving the correct paperwork, two tests had been approved. One of these was a test developed by the CDC. The first batch of CDC kits didn't work for numerous labs and contributed to the country's testing problems.

Critics of the CDC, including some doctors, said the organization's criteria for who could be tested hid the true extent of the COVID-19 pandemic in the United States. "We didn't detect it because we weren't testing properly. There may have been cryptic transmission in Washington

State since January. If I sound alarmed, it's because I am," tweeted Matthew McCarthy, a hospital physician at Weill Cornell Medicine in New York City.[4] In January, by CDC criteria, patients had to have traveled to Wuhan, China, or been in contact with someone with a positive COVID-19 test result to be tested themselves. In March, these criteria expanded to include travel to other hot spots. By the end of March, the CDC expanded its guidelines to include health-care providers, first responders, people in hospitals or other care facilities, and anyone else as determined by state or local health departments. This meant US testing criteria varied from state to state.

WIDESPREAD TESTING

While some countries tested only limited numbers of people, others, including Iceland, took a more widespread approach. The Icelandic government said it tested a higher proportion of its 364,000-person population than any other country. By March 2020, Iceland had tested 3,787 people. This translates to roughly 10,405 people per million, compared with South Korea's roughly 5,203 per million, Italy's 2,478 per million, and the United Kingdom's

MORE TO THE
STORY

TESTING NUMBERS

Comparing testing numbers is tricky. As of April 2020, the United States had tested 3.9 million people. That sounds like a lot, but the United States also has a higher population than many other countries. That is why this data is frequently reported as tests per million people.

By April 20, 2020, the United States had tested 11,821 people per million, up from five people per million in early March. Italy was still ahead of the United States at 20,926 tests per million, while South Korea had tested 10,862 people per million.[5] Harvard University researchers explained that in late April, the United States was testing an average of 146,000 people per day. They recommended that number reach 500,000 to 700,000 tests per day before social distancing restrictions be relaxed.[6]

764 per million at that time.[7] Of the 3,787 people tested in Iceland, 218 tests came back positive, and at least half of these people contracted the virus while traveling in other parts of Europe.[8] Icelandic health officials said they planned to eventually test everyone.

Unlike many countries, Iceland tested people who showed no COVID-19 symptoms. "Early results . . . indicate that a low proportion of the general population has contracted the virus and that about half of those who tested positive are non-symptomatic. The other half displays very moderate cold-like symptoms," said Thorolfur Gudnason, Iceland's chief epidemiologist.[9] This offered scientists insight into the number of people who are infected but show no symptoms. Once researchers know what portion of the population is made up of asymptomatic individuals, they can use the numbers of symptomatic positive tests to estimate how many more people are sick but show no symptoms. This can help scientists estimate how many people in various countries have actually been infected.

"[ICELAND'S TESTING] EFFORT IS INTENDED TO GATHER INSIGHT INTO THE ACTUAL PREVALENCE OF THE VIRUS IN THE COMMUNITY."[10]

—THOROLFUR GUDNASON, ICELAND'S CHIEF EPIDEMIOLOGIST, 2020

FROM THE
HEADLINES

FALSE POSITIVES AND BAD TESTS

In addition to limited access to testing, problems arose when COVID-19 tests were not accurate. This is what happened with the first batch of tests sent out by the CDC to 50 labs.[11] When the labs ran a test to make sure everything was working correctly, most got negative results, showing their test kits weren't working. The problem was found to be contaminated reagents, the chemicals used in the kits to test for the virus. Polymerase chain reaction tests are extremely sensitive, and problems are not unusual. This is why the kits are tested before being used on patients. But to have the problem occur on this scale, when testing and tracking infected people would have made a big difference early in the pandemic, meant there would be much higher numbers of infected people.

Governments around the world also sought antibody tests so that their people could leave social isolation and go back to work. But experts warned of the dangerous potential for inaccuracy in early COVID-19 antibody tests. False positives on

A lab technician prepares patient samples for COVID-19 testing.

antibody tests would show that people have antibodies when they do not. If numerous people without antibodies moved around and became infected, the virus could spread further. Some antibody tests required only a finger prick to put blood on a test strip instead of the usual method of taking blood from a vein. "From a technological perspective, with a test using a finger prick, you will never get as good a result as if you take the blood from the vein," said Thomas Schinecker, diagnostic chief of Roche, a Swiss health-care company. "I would take those results with caution."[12]

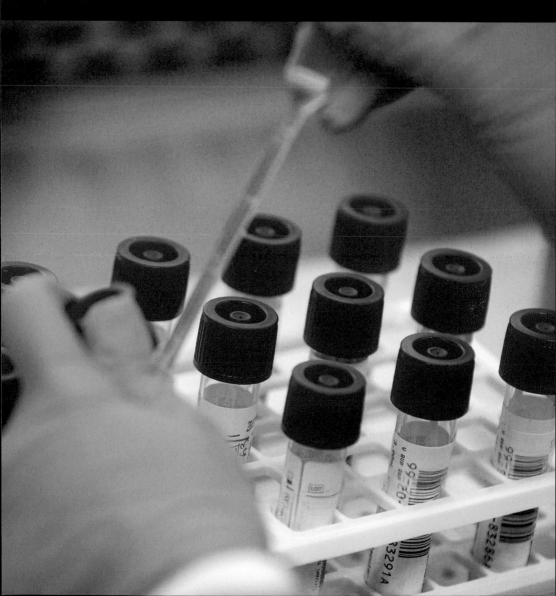

CHAPTER SIX

TREATING
COVID-19

With no cure, treating COVID-19 meant treating the symptoms. People who were running fevers and coughing were told to isolate themselves at home. If they lived with other people, this meant remaining alone in a room for approximately two weeks and using a bathroom, if possible, that no one else used. When they had to be around people, such as when visiting a doctor, they had to wear a mask.

For aches and pains as well as fever, people could take over-the-counter medications such as acetaminophen or ibuprofen. Cough syrups and other cough suppressing medications were prescribed. Patients were told to get plenty of rest, drink fluids, and

Patients recovering from COVID-19 symptoms at home were told to stay as isolated as possible.

eat nutritious foods to help their immune systems fight the illness.

Very sick people, such as those with advanced pneumonia or organ failure, had to be admitted to hospitals. Those with severe pneumonia were given oxygen. In areas that were especially hard hit, hospitals filled quickly and ventilators were in short supply. Health-care professionals worked to provide whatever treatment they could. Various companies partnered to produce more ventilators, and temporary hospitals were set up around the world. Meanwhile, scientists also worked to develop specific COVID-19 treatments—antiviral drugs, antibody treatments, and vaccines.

ANTIVIRALS

One of the first things scientists and doctors do when seeking treatments for a new

TEMPORARY HOSPITALS

As the numbers of COVID-19 patients increased, officials had to find creative solutions to try to avoid hospital overcrowding. In the United States, two navy hospital ships were deployed. The USNS *Comfort* served New York and the USNS *Mercy* served Los Angeles, California. Tent hospitals went up in New York City's Central Park and in Lombard, Italy. Hotels, conference centers, and sports stadiums were reconfigured to hold patients in the United States, Spain, Brazil, and China. Sometimes these temporary hospitals were for non-coronavirus patients, freeing up hospital beds for COVID-19 patients.

virus is to look for solutions among existing drugs. For SARS-CoV-2, these included antivirals, which are drugs that prevent a virus from reproducing. Two that have been tried experimentally for COVID-19 are remdesivir and leronlimab. Leronlimab has also been tested to treat AIDS patients. In AIDS patients, the drug binds onto specific cells to prevent infection, reducing the spread of the virus. Two groups of COVID-19 patients, including ten people in New York City, were given leronlimab in early 2020. Some patients were able to come off the ventilators after receiving the drug. Further testing was needed before leronlimab could be widely administered to COVID-19 patients.

Remdesivir was developed to treat viral infections including Ebola and coronaviruses. It mimics a molecule that these viruses need to duplicate, disrupts the molecule's replication, and reduces the spread of the virus. A month-long trial of the drug on Chinese COVID-19 patients was disappointing—13.9 percent of remdesivir patients died while 12.8 percent of placebo patients died.[1] A longer study may have yielded different results, but the number of volunteer patients declined as the number of infections in China declined. A National Institutes of Health (NIH) trial showed that remdesivir reduced recovery time from 15 to 11 days.[2] Based on that NIH trial, on May 1, 2020, the FDA approved remdesivir as emergency treatment for hospitalized COVID-19 patients in the United States. Japan's government approved similar use of the drug shortly after the United States did, and the United Kingdom followed suit in late May. Meanwhile, researchers continued investigating whether remdesivir caused irregular heartbeat in some patients. In early June, India and South Korea approved emergency use of remdesivir for COVID-19.

In addition to antiviral drugs, scientists also studied steroid drug treatments for COVID-19 patients. An Oxford University study showed in June 2020 that the steroid dexamethasone significantly reduced deaths among severely ill COVID-19 patients. Some hospitals were hesitant to administer this treatment because of concerns about how steroids affect people's immune systems. But other hospitals began to increase their use of dexamethasone.

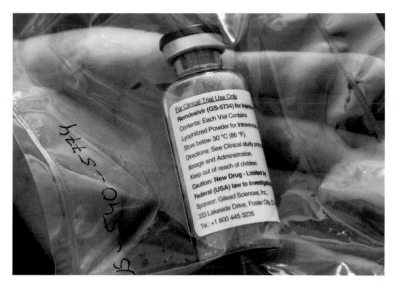

Remdesivir is administered to patients through injection.

ANTIBODY TREATMENTS

Researchers also worked on new treatments. David Ho, the
scientist who developed the AIDS treatment, worked with
his team of scientists to develop a new antibody treatment
for COVID-19. The treatment would keep the coronavirus
from entering cells. Ho's goal was to find a treatment
that could be delivered in pill form. Ho's team included
Alejandro Chavez, an assistant professor of pathology and
biology at New York City's Columbia University. Chavez
developed a method to test possible drugs on dozens of
different coronaviruses at one time. The team hoped to
use this method to identify treatments effective against
more than one coronavirus.

Regeneron Pharmaceuticals Inc., a biotech company in New York, also worked on a COVID-19 antibody treatment. The company had previously developed an Ebola antibody treatment. Its COVID-19 treatment would have to be injected, making it more complicated than taking a pill.

VACCINES

When a virus or bacterium enters a person's body, the immune system knows it is an invader because its arrangement of proteins is not recognized by the body. The immune system fights it off with protein molecules called antibodies. A vaccine also triggers the production of antibodies, preparing the body for the next fight. A vaccine keeps people from becoming reinfected if they again encounter the same virus.

On April 9, 2020, the journal *Nature Reviews Drug Discovery* released a list of ongoing research to create a COVID-19 vaccine. There were 115 programs on the list. Different companies worked on different types of vaccines. Live attenuated vaccines contain a live, weakened virus that will create immunity but not lead to an infection. Other vaccines contain inactivated virus that has been treated with disinfectants to keep the vaccine from creating an infection while still allowing antibodies to be produced. Other vaccines use only the virus's DNA, its RNA, or a fragment of its proteins. The most effective vaccines use live virus.

These companies were working quickly. A COVID-19 vaccine developed by Moderna, a Massachusetts biotech company, was ready to be tested on humans in early March 2020. This was possible because it was an RNA vaccine, which are quicker to develop than other vaccines. Moderna was also allowed to skip animal testing, a step normally taken before testing on human subjects. The company skipped this step because scientists did not yet know which animals were the original hosts of the virus and thus might be susceptible to infection. SARS-CoV-2 seemed to have little effect on lab mice.

US president Donald Trump hoped to have a vaccine available to Americans by the end of 2020.

"SOME VIRUSES ARE VERY, VERY DIFFICULT WHEN IT COMES TO VACCINE DEVELOPMENT—SO FOR THE FORESEEABLE FUTURE, WE ARE GOING TO HAVE TO FIND WAYS TO GO ABOUT OUR LIVES WITH THIS VIRUS AS A CONSTANT THREAT."[3]

—DAVID NABARRO, PROFESSOR OF GLOBAL HEALTH, IMPERIAL COLLEGE LONDON, 2020

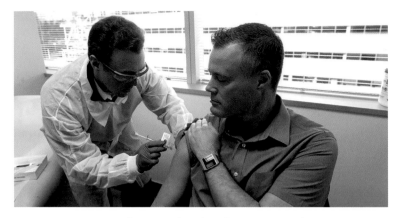

A patient receives a shot in a clinical trial for a potential COVID-19 vaccine in March 2020.

Moderna was among five companies identified by Trump's administration in June 2020 as most likely to produce a successful vaccine for COVID-19. The other companies were Johnson & Johnson, Merck, Pfizer, and AstraZeneca.

Normally a vaccine takes ten to twenty years to produce. Ethics experts worried about the risks of rushing development of a COVID-19 vaccine. "We may not be able to minimize the risks as much as we would hope to, because we have the time pressure of the outbreak," said Holly Fernandez Lynch, assistant professor of medical ethics at the University of Pennsylvania.[4] One concern is the risk of vaccine enhancement, which is when vaccinated patients are not immune but actually more susceptible to the virus. Scientists don't fully understand why vaccine enhancement can occur, but testing for this problem is one reason why vaccines typically take a long time to develop.

In April 2020, Christopher Whitty, the United Kingdom's chief medical officer, warned his country's government that a vaccine for COVID-19 may never be found. One concern, he said, was the fact that scientists remained uncertain about whether COVID-19 patients developed long-term immunity after recovering from the disease. "If we don't [know that], then it doesn't make a vaccine impossible, but it makes it much less likely, and we simply don't know yet," Whitty said.[5] Attempts to create other coronavirus vaccines have failed. "Vaccines are looked for, for every infectious disease. They are not found for all of them," he said.[6]

MEDICAL WORKERS

With emergency rooms and intensive care units (ICUs) filling up, medical staff were extremely stressed during the COVID-19 pandemic. The Medical Center in Aurora, Colorado, normally has a maximum of 38 ICU patients. But during the pandemic, it expanded into two additional parts of the hospital to house 50 ICU patients.[7] These patients require more care than non-ICU patients, and having them in numerous areas makes their care even more difficult. Normally friends and family bolster the spirits of critically ill patients, but hospital visitors were banned during the pandemic as part of social distancing measures. This meant hospital staff had to communicate medical information by phone to family members. They helped families speak to patients through video chat. Although a patient with a ventilator cannot speak, they can be encouraged by family members. Health-care workers were also often the only people at the bedsides of dying COVID-19 patients. These workers rose to the challenges in caring for their patients during the pandemic.

Some researchers noted that SARS-CoV-2 had been mutating slowly, which could help in developing a vaccine. "The virus has had very few genetic changes since it emerged in late 2019. Designing vaccines and therapeutics for a single strain is much more straightforward than [for] a virus that is changing quickly," said Peter Thielen, a molecular biologist who studied the virus on a team at Johns Hopkins University.[8]

STUDYING RECOVERED PATIENTS

As the pandemic progressed, medical researchers began studying the antibody-rich blood of people who recovered from COVID-19 or who were exposed to the virus. Some doctors experimented with using the blood of people who had recovered from COVID-19 in a treatment called convalescent plasma therapy. They hoped this treatment could help people with severe cases of COVID-19. In this treatment, plasma, a part of blood that contains fluid and antibodies but no red blood cells, is slowly delivered through an intravenous line directly into a person's vein. Researchers hoped the plasma could boost patients' immune systems enough to fight off COVID-19.

Blood samples were also used to study the genes of Spanish and Italian COVID-19 patients on ventilators to see whether there was any genetic commonality in these severe cases. A group of European researchers found that the ventilator patients had some genes in common, including the gene that determines blood type. Patients with type A blood were 50 percent more likely to need help getting oxygen.[9] This indicates that people with type A blood may be more vulnerable to severe COVID-19 symptoms. As people continued to become infected and recover from COVID-19, medical researchers continued their studies in hopes of finding more effective treatments or a vaccine for the disease.

OVERWHELMED HOSPITALS

New York City was among the hardest hit places during the pandemic. The city's hospitals became overwhelmed by the high number of COVID-19 patients. One of these hospitals, Brookdale University Hospital Medical Center, normally has about 300 patients. By the end of March 2020 it had exceeded this number and needed to reopen floors that had been closed. Doctors in New York City hospitals worked to avoid decisions about which patients would get ventilators. Hospitals brought older ventilators back into use and also adapted anesthesia machines to deliver oxygen. Still, many patients died. As hospital morgues were designed to hold only 20 dead people, refrigerated trailers were parked outside various hospitals to be used as makeshift morgues.[10] By June 1, 2020, the COVID-19 death toll for New York City, both those who had died at home and in hospitals, had reached 16,882.[11]

FROM THE
HEADLINES

MAKING VENTILATORS

Delivering oxygen to people who are fighting to breathe is one of the trickiest problems in treating COVID-19 patients, and it often requires a ventilator. After news reports surfaced about Italian doctors running out of ventilators and having to decide which patients would get to use the lifesaving machines, British government officials wanted to be prepared for a similar situation in their own country. They approached the company Dyson and asked it to design a ventilator. In ten days, Dyson, which normally manufactures vacuum cleaners, air filters, and hand dryers, came back with the design for a small mobile ventilator that would fasten onto a bed rail. Smaller than many hospital ventilators and battery powered, it would be easy to use in temporary hospitals. In addition to the ventilators ordered by the British government, Dyson planned to make 4,000 ventilators for other countries.[12]

US automobile manufacturers also started making ventilators. General Motors (GM) worked with Ventec to build the company's VOCSN ventilator model, an FDA-approved design. Because Ventec already made this ventilator, production could begin quickly. GM's manufacturing plant in Kokomo, Indiana, was chosen for the job because it normally does advanced electronic work and was able to apply this to making the ventilators. Ford worked with GE Healthcare to build Model-A, another FDA-approved ventilator.

In addition to producing hospital ventilators, General Motors had some of its factory technicians repair ventilators.

CHAPTER SEVEN

ECONOMIC
IMPACT

As governments in US states and in countries around the world issued stay-at-home orders, people could only venture out for essential reasons, including for doctor's appointments and to purchase food. With so many people staying home all the time, many businesses began to suffer. The airline industry saw dramatic decreases in revenue as many people avoided flying during the pandemic. Hotels saw a similar decline due to reduced travel. Restaurants, cinemas, amusement parks, and sports venues all saw their revenue drop as people stayed home. Governments even forced many of these places to close temporarily to prevent people from gathering.

Many businesses temporarily closed during the pandemic.

The widespread lack of spending plunged the world into a recession.

A recession is a period of declining economic activity that lasts for at least six months. The affected economic activity may be manufacturing, employment, or retail spending. Economic experts predicted the recession spurred by COVID-19 would be at least as bad as the Great Recession, which lasted from 2007 to 2009. Yet in many ways, the coronavirus recession was different than all preceding recessions because of its sudden nature. As the pandemic quickly spread, spending halted abruptly. Typically, the decline in spending or earning leading up to a recession is more gradual.

THE GREAT RECESSION

The Great Recession began in 2007. In the years leading up to it, the US government wanted to encourage homeownership, so the Federal Reserve Bank encouraged low-interest loans. Home buyers took out larger loans and bought bigger houses than they might have otherwise, and banks made a lot of these loans. When housing prices dropped, people still had to pay back their loans, although the houses they were paying for were worth much less. When people couldn't make their payments, banks took their houses. But then the banks couldn't sell the homes, and they were unable to recover what was still owed on the loans. The financial repercussions of this crisis started in the United States but, with so many banks operating internationally, they soon impacted the world economy.

FLUCTUATIONS

One of the first indicators of the coronavirus recession was a drop in US stock prices at the end of February 2020. At the time, not many people realized COVID-19 was already in the United States. But investors were watching the impact of the virus overseas and predicted the virus would eventually impact US businesses. When people are worried about bad business conditions, they worry about the money they have invested in various businesses. This is because poor business conditions often mean that a business drops in value. When this happens, its investors lose money. As COVID-19 spread, investors' confidence dropped further. Worried about continued losses, they sold their stocks to limit their losses.

"People are trading stocks with their cellphones on their living room couches with the television news blaring about the pandemic," Robert Shiller, an economist at Yale University, said in April 2020. "There is widespread foreboding, not just about the economy but about the possibility of grave illness or death in the weeks ahead."[1]

When many stocks are sold at one time, their prices can fall even further.

Oil prices also fell during the recession. In the United Kingdom and the United States, they hit the lowest price seen in 18 years.[2] This was largely because demand fell as people stayed home and drove less, reducing the amount of fuel needed at that time.

Although people were selling stocks and not gassing up their cars, they were buying more of certain products. For example, before the COVID-19 pandemic, orange juice sales had dropped steadily, partly because health-conscious people worried that fruit juice might be too sugary and full of calories. But during the pandemic, people throughout the United States stocked their pantries and refrigerators in anticipation of staying home. As orange juice, a source of vitamin C, is thought to help fight off illnesses, sales of orange juice jumped 38 percent in March 2020.[3]

JOBLESSNESS

When businesses closed as a result of social distancing regulations, many of them laid off or furloughed their employees, leading to an increase in unemployed workers across the United States. In April 2020 alone, 20.5 million Americans lost their jobs.[5]

Unemployment checks are sent out by state governments as a way to help replace part of people's normal income while they look for work. Unemployment checks only cover a percentage of a person's regular salary, and the amount varies from state to state. Mississippi pays an average of 31 percent of a recipient's normal wages,

A worker at Mississippi's state unemployment office takes a woman's application for unemployment payments in April 2020.

while Massachusetts pays an average of 43 percent.[6]

On March 27, 2020, the US Congress passed a $2 trillion aid package, called the Coronavirus Aid, Relief, and Economic Security (CARES) Act, and part of this package was an additional $600 per week to each unemployment recipient. The goal was to ensure that people who were unemployed could survive without their regular income.

The economic downturn did force some businesses to close permanently. But because this recession was caused by a health threat, economic experts hoped that with government aid sustaining them during the crisis, most temporarily closed businesses would eventually reopen. Then people would return to their jobs.

The CARES Act included more than just payments to the unemployed. There was also a one-time economic stimulus check of $1,200

UNEMPLOYMENT

In addition to adding to weekly checks received on unemployment, the CARES Act also expanded who was eligible to receive unemployment payments. Those previously ineligible who could receive payments during the crisis included self-employed people, gig workers such as Uber and Lyft drivers, and furloughed employees. Those who did not qualify in the past earned 50 percent of their individual state's normal unemployment payout, plus the additional $600 per week. Previously, people could collect unemployment for only 26 weeks, but the CARES Act expanded this to up to 39 weeks.[7]

to most US adults, with the amount varying based on income. There were also loans available to big businesses such as airlines and hotels, as well as $377 billion dedicated to loans for small businesses. The package also included $100 billion in assistance for US hospitals and health-care systems overwhelmed by the numbers of patients, $30 billion in education funding to help supplement strained state budgets, and $25 billion for public transportation systems to help compensate for a drop in ridership when schools and businesses closed.

GOVERNMENT IMPACT

The recession affected state and local governments differently than the federal government. As people earn less and spend less, governments earn less in tax revenues. At the same time, the pandemic created higher demand for some government services, such as government health insurance and unemployment payments. While the federal government can run a deficit, spending more than it makes in taxes and other revenues, state and local governments have less flexibility to do this. This means that spending may have to be cut in other areas, such as education, transportation, or parks.

CHAPTER EIGHT

RACIAL AND
CULTURAL
DISPARITIES

As US cities and states collected data on COVID-19 patients by race, discouraging trends appeared. A disproportionate number of people of color were getting sick. By June 2020, Black people in Washington State comprised 7 percent of COVID-19 patients but only 4 percent of the total population. Latinx people made up 39 percent of COVID-19 patients but only 13 percent of the population.[1] At that same time in Illinois, Black people made up 17 percent of COVID-19 patients but 14 percent of the population, while Latinx people constituted 31 percent of COVID-19 patients compared with 17 percent of the population.[2]

COVID-19 disproportionately affected Black people in the United States.

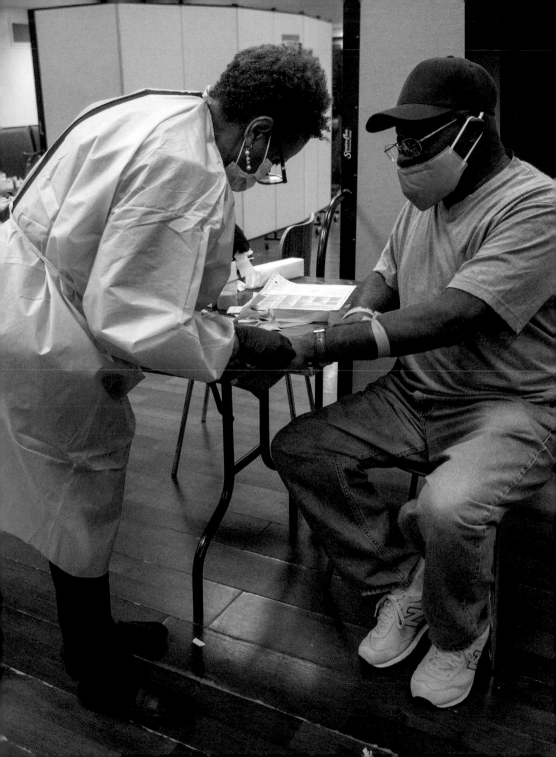

Coronavirus experts said people of color are not inherently more likely to become infected. Part of the problem is that many preexisting conditions that make people more susceptible to COVID-19 are more prevalent among Latinx and Black Americans, who often face barriers in accessing quality health care. "We have known literally forever that diseases like diabetes, hypertension, obesity, and asthma are disproportionately afflicting the minority populations, particularly the African Americans," said Dr. Anthony Fauci, the top US advisor on infectious diseases.[3] Fauci stated that a crisis, such as a pandemic, often makes societal weaknesses obvious. "When all of this is over—and as we said, it will end, we will get over coronavirus—but there will still be health disparities which we really need to address in the African American community," Fauci said.[4]

POVERTY MATTERS

As it became clear how dangerous COVID-19 was, businesses around the world enabled employees to work from home whenever possible. But many people could not work from home, particularly those in low-income jobs.

MORE TO THE
STORY

MISSING INFORMATION?

The Indian Health Service (IHS) is the federal agency responsible for tracking Native American health issues in the United States. About one-sixth of the country's 423 Native American–focused health facilities are run by the IHS.[5] The rest are operated by tribal governments or intertribal organizations, which can report their data but often don't. This lack of information is critical because Native Americans have a lower life expectancy and larger numbers of respiratory problems than the general population. Both factors put them at greater risk of death if they become ill with COVID-19.

On Native American reservations, one out of every six homes is overcrowded, which means disease can spread more easily. According to the US Department of Housing and Urban Development, a home is considered overcrowded if there are more people than there are rooms. A four-room home with six people living in it is overcrowded, by definition, even if it is a traditional, multigenerational family. In addition to overcrowding, in some remote areas, there is no plumbing, which limits handwashing. "There's no mystery as to why Indian Country suffers from health disparities that are alarming and shocking, even when there isn't a pandemic running across the globe. We're in a very precarious situation right now," Kevin Allis, CEO of the National Congress of American Indians, said in March 2020.[6]

Among those less likely to be able to work from home were many Black and Latinx people.

The US Bureau of Labor Statistics collected data that showed that less than 20 percent of Black workers and about 16 percent of Latinx workers were able to telecommute. This compares with 37 percent of Asian workers and 30 percent of white workers who reported they could telecommute.[7] In addition, when asked by the Pew Research Center, about 66 percent of Latinx adults said that if they had to miss work for two weeks because of the coronavirus, they would not get paid. "African Americans and Latinos and other minority groups are the ones out there in the warehouse, emptying food trucks, delivering your Grubhub or Uber Eats," said Stephen Thomas, director of the Maryland Center for Health Equity at the University of Maryland School of Public Health.[8] Thomas emphasized that this puts them at greater risk of contracting COVID-19.

In early April, data by race from New York City COVID-19 cases was made available, and New York governor Andrew Cuomo didn't like what he saw. Although Black people composed only 22 percent of the population, they made up 28 percent of the deaths. The Latinx population was similarly misrepresented, at 29 percent of the population but 34 percent of the deaths.[10] "Why is it that the poorest people always pay the highest price? Are more public workers Latino and African American? Who don't have a choice, frankly, but to go out there every day and drive the bus and drive the train and show up for work and wind up subjecting themselves to, in this case, the virus?" he said.[11] Cuomo demanded increased COVID-19 testing for people of color and more research on the situation in general.

HUNGER BY THE NUMBERS

On an average school day, 29.7 million schoolchildren, many from low-income families, get free or reduced-rate lunches at school. In addition, 14.6 million students a day eat breakfast at school. But with schools across the United States closed, school district nutritionists had to find another way to get those meals to children who may otherwise go hungry. This became especially important as the number of people applying for unemployment increased, because a lack of income affected parents' ability to feed their children. School districts have taken a variety of approaches to this issue. Some made meals available for no-contact pickup in parking lots. Other districts used school buses to deliver meals.[12]

Another issue is that viruses, including SARS-CoV-2, spread more easily and more rapidly where people live close together. The Pew Research Center studied demographic data, finding that Black people are more likely to live in crowded cities rather than in suburbs or rural areas, where homes are farther apart. The racial disparity in income means that Black people are also more likely to live in smaller, more crowded apartments or homes.

Not only does this mean that low-income people are more likely to contract the virus but also that they are more likely to infect other people. Health-care officials stated that people who may have COVID-19 should isolate themselves from others. This is impossible for many living in apartment buildings or homeless

COVID-19 IN PRISONS

In May 2020, approximately 2.2 million people lived in US prisons. Close living quarters are assumed to allow the disease to spread easily, putting these prisoners at high risk. "Prisoners share toilets, bathrooms, sinks, and dining halls. They are mostly sleeping in bunk beds," said Frederick Altice of the Yale School of Medicine. "These settings are in no way equipped to deal with an outbreak once it gets in."[13] The *Marshall Project*, a nonprofit news organization that tracks information on the US criminal justice system, reported that by April 22, 2020, at least 9,437 American prisoners had COVID-19 and at least 131 had died from the disease.[14]

shelters. The space is not available for them to take this precaution, and this makes the virus more likely to spread.

COMMUNICATION PROBLEMS

Approximately 25 million people in the United States speak little or no English.[15] This language barrier may limit people's understanding of public health messages sent out by governments. This includes messages about social distancing and other COVID-19 rules or resources.

Some hospital workers were able to video chat with translators to help COVID-19 patients who did not speak English.

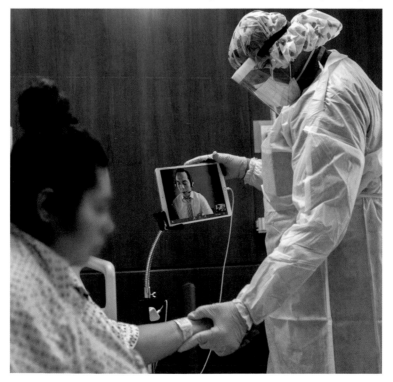

Language barriers can also limit people's ability to seek medical help, especially if a hospital doesn't have a translator readily available.

But language has not been the only communication problem during the pandemic. Local businesses, churches, and other neighborhood places where people gather had to close because of social distancing guidelines. In some neighborhoods, people may not look to public health authorities as the most trusted source of information. Instead, they rely on connecting with neighbors in these gathering spaces to learn about what's happening in the community. When businesses and other places are forced to close, these sources of information are no longer available. "Who's making sure that they have the information, the

RACE RUMORS

When actor Idris Elba, who is Black, announced on social media that he had been diagnosed with COVID-19, he was appalled by some of the comments he read. "There are so many stupid, ridiculous conspiracy theories about Black people not being able to get it. . . . That is the quickest way to get more Black people killed," Elba said in March 2020.[16] That same month, rapper Waka Flocka Flame, who is also Black, appeared on a radio show and said, "Minorities can't catch coronavirus. Name one. It doesn't touch them soul food folks."[17] False rumors circulated that the melanin in Black and brown people's skin protected them from the virus. Disinformation and bad science during a pandemic may cause people to unintentionally endanger themselves because they believe they can't get sick.

evidence-based information, to help dispel myths, to shut down conspiracy theories and to ensure that African Americans recognize, 'Hey, this disease is affecting us'?" Stephen Thomas said.[18]

Many local governments have community liaison programs to reach out to various populations. These liaisons typically speak more than one language. Some cities began using these programs to help communicate information related to the COVID-19 pandemic. When Salt Lake City, Utah, mayor Jenny Wilson saw that her county's Latinx population was hit hard by COVID-19, she formed the Equity for Diverse and Underserved Communities Team. The group included a communications specialist to make sure people received accurate information. It also included a business liaison to help business owners apply for available funding.

CHAPTER NINE

THE
FUTURE

By the last week of May 2020, all 50 US states were reopening, meaning they began lifting many of the restrictions established by their stay-at-home orders. Government leaders felt pressured to let people get back to work to reinvigorate city and state economies. Yet health officials warned that as social distancing was relaxed, more people would get sick with COVID-19.

Plans to reopen varied from state to state, and most reopened gradually. For example, there were still restrictions on how many customers could be at certain businesses and public spaces at one time. Many places still had rules about cleanliness, wearing face masks, and social distancing.

As businesses reopened, they had special rules about cleanliness and other guidelines to continue reducing the spread of COVID-19.

Not all states waited to reopen until their numbers of infections declined. In North Carolina, Democratic governor Roy Cooper signed an executive order to reopen restaurants, hair salons, tattoo parlors, and swimming pools at half capacity. Cooper said he made the decision because, although diagnosed cases were still increasing, the number of COVID-19 emergency room visits and hospitalized patients had dropped. "I'm glad the governor responded to the calls of senators, small-business owners, and unemployed workers to let them get back to work," said Republican state senate leader Phil Berger.[1]

"IT ISN'T GOING TO BE POSSIBLE FOR US TO TRULY BE ABLE TO RETURN TO NORMAL UNTIL WE HAVE A VACCINE."[2]

—WINSTON TIMP, ASSISTANT PROFESSOR OF BIOMEDICAL ENGINEERING AT JOHNS HOPKINS UNIVERSITY, JUNE 2020

SECOND WAVE

Public health officials warned that reopening too early would lead to a second wave of COVID-19 infections. On May 21, 2020, when asked during a visit to Michigan about a possible second wave, President Trump acknowledged it could happen. "We're not going to close the country;

we're going to put out the fires. Whether it's an ember or a flame, we're going to put it out," Trump said.[3]

By early July, states across the country had started to see increased case numbers after reopening. In response, some states, including Florida and Texas, began closing bars again. Arizona governor Doug Ducey closed bars, gyms, movie theaters, and water parks. Other states, including Kansas and Oregon, issued statewide orders requiring people to wear masks in public spaces.

Officials continued telling people to wear face masks in public as many places around the world, including South Korea, began to reopen.

Meanwhile, health officials urged more government leaders to take action to reduce the spread of the virus.

A second wave of infections also hit South Korea after parts of the country reopened. On May 29, 2020, thousands of South Korean students returned to school, but the next day 79 new cases were reported, the highest count for a single day in two months.[4] Most were linked to a warehouse and distribution center in the city of Bucheon. South Korean officials discovered that the facility had not followed infection control measures. Just days after reopening, 251 schools in the city were closed again. Meanwhile, Seoul, the country's capital, delayed opening its schools. Although Bucheon's spike in infections was caused by just one warehouse that did not follow the rules, South Korean officials decided that continuing with reopening would only make the situation worse.

A variety of factors can lead to a second wave. If people stop social distancing when the basic reproduction number is too high, infections will climb. Another factor that could lead to a second wave is lack of immunity. Models used to project how many COVID-19 cases would occur in the future often assumed that a person who had recovered would be immune. But as scientists continued studying the virus, they were uncertain how much immunity COVID-19 patients actually developed after recovering. If there were not enough immune people for herd immunity and people stopped social distancing, experts believed that a second wave would occur.

Although COVID-19 was first detected at the Wuhan market in China, it spread around the world.

ANOTHER CORONAVIRUS

Scientists such as David Ho believe the world has not seen its last coronavirus pandemic. "Surely there will be another one. This is the third outbreak in two decades," said Ho, referring to SARS, MERS, and COVID-19.[5]

In an interview with *Bloomberg Businessweek*, Ho mentioned bats make up one-fifth of mammal species. Bats, which live in many different places around the world, carry viruses that have infected humans. "There are so many viruses that reside in bats—SARS and Ebola and perhaps this coronavirus [SARS-CoV-2]," Ho said.[6] As people continue to build in wild habitats, they come into contact with animals and the viruses they carry. One of these viruses could become a pandemic.

CONTINUING TO SPREAD

Throughout 2020, COVID-19 continued to spread around the world. After widely infecting people throughout East Asia, Europe, and the Americas, COVID-19 case numbers began rising across Africa in May 2020. The Africa Centres for Disease Control and Prevention reported more than 115,000 cases with more than 3,400 deaths across the continent by May 26, 2020.[7]

People were especially worried about refugee camps in South Sudan, where 1.5 million people lived crowded together.[8] Health officials knew that in crowded places where people have limited clean water and receive poor health care, the virus spread more quickly. They also knew the virus could once again spread through communities, as happened when infections spiked in Wuhan and later throughout China. Until a vaccine or effective treatment could be developed, COVID-19 was expected to be a lingering threat around the world.

ESSENTIAL
FACTS

MAJOR EVENTS

- On December 31, 2019, Chinese health officials contact the World Health Organization (WHO) to report multiple cases of viral pneumonia in the city of Wuhan.

- On January 9, 2020, the WHO reports that the Chinese pneumonia patients were infected by a novel coronavirus, later named SARS-CoV-2. The disease caused by this virus was later named COVID-19.

- On January 19, 2020, a man who had visited family in Wuhan goes to a clinic in Snohomish County, Washington State. He becomes the first confirmed COVID-19 patient in the United States.

- By January 20, 2020, COVID-19 cases are reported in several other countries including Japan, South Korea, and Thailand.

- On March 11, 2020, the WHO declares COVID-19 a pandemic.

- On April 3, 2020, the CDC recommends that people in the United States wear face masks when in public.

KEY PLAYERS

- Dr. Li Wenliang warned fellow doctors about the novel coronavirus and was reprimanded by the Chinese government. He later contracted the virus and died of COVID-19 on February 7, 2020.

- David Ho was one of the first scientists to begin work on an antiviral drug to combat the novel coronavirus.

- Scientist Olfert Landt made one of the first tests to determine whether a person was infected with COVID-19.

- Dr. Helen Chu led a research team that conducted COVID-19 tests in the Seattle area without permission. The tests crucially identified the first US hot spot, in March 2020.

IMPACT ON SOCIETY

As COVID-19 spread worldwide, several million people were infected, and hundreds of thousands of people died. With so many people sick, health-care systems around the world were under enormous strain. The hardest-hit regions struggled to find hospital beds and medical personnel to treat the critically ill. In addition, economic activity dropped as people took shelter in their homes to avoid becoming sick and spreading the virus. Meanwhile, scientists worked to find a treatment or vaccine to stop the virus.

QUOTE

"Vaccines are looked for, for every infectious disease. They are not found for all of them."

—UK chief medical officer Christopher Whitty, 2020

GLOSSARY

ASYMPTOMATIC
Not showing signs of an infection.

BIOTECH
A company that uses living organisms or other biological systems in the manufacture of drugs or other products.

DISPARITY
A great difference.

EPIDEMIC
The rapid spreading of a disease so that many people have it at the same time.

EPIDEMIOLOGIST
A scientist who studies how diseases occur, spread, and can be controlled in a population.

FURLOUGH
To make someone take a temporary unpaid leave of absence or time off from work, often for a set period of time.

LAY OFF

To suspend an employee from work without pay or other benefits, usually permanently.

OUTBREAK

A sudden rise in the occurrence of a disease.

PANDEMIC

The worldwide spread of a disease.

QUARANTINE

To physically isolate, particularly for people who are ill and possibly contagious.

REVENUE

Income, especially of a company or organization and of a substantial nature.

TELECOMMUTE

To work from home and connect with coworkers online or by phone.

VACCINE

A drug that prevents or treats illness by stimulating the immune system to create antibodies or by blocking the effects of a substance.

VIROLOGIST

A scientist who studies viruses and the diseases caused by these microorganisms.

ADDITIONAL
RESOURCES

SELECTED BIBLIOGRAPHY

Cuthbert, Lori. "How Do Infections Like the Coronavirus Jump from Animals to People?" *National Geographic*, 1 Apr. 2020, nationalgeographic.com. Accessed 11 May 2020.

Gibbens, Sarah. "Why Soap Is Preferable to Bleach in the Fight against Coronavirus." *National Geographic*, 18 Mar. 2020, nationalgeographic.com. Accessed 11 May 2020.

Horiuchi, Vince. "Mucus and the Coronavirus." *@theU, University of Utah*, 31 Mar. 2020, attheu.utah.edu. Accessed 11 May 2020.

FURTHER READINGS

Laine, Carolee. *Ebola Outbreak*. Abdo, 2016.

Marrin, Albert. *Very, Very, Very Dreadful: The Influenza Pandemic of 1918*. Alfred A. Knopf, 2018.

Rissman, Rebecca. *The Vaccination Debate*. Abdo, 2016.

ONLINE RESOURCES

To learn more about the COVID-19 pandemic, please visit **abdobooklinks.com** or scan this QR code. These links are routinely monitored and updated to provide the most current information available.

MORE INFORMATION

For more information on this subject, contact or visit the following organizations:

US Centers for Disease Control and Prevention
1600 Clifton Rd.
Atlanta, GA 30329
800-232-4636
cdc.gov
The CDC is part of the US Department of Health and Human Services. The organization's goal is to protect the health and safety of US residents, including during the COVID-19 pandemic.

World Health Organization
525 Twenty-Third St. NW
Washington, DC 20037
202-974-3000
who.int
A part of the United Nations, the WHO focuses on global health and finding solutions to health issues that cross national borders, such as pandemics. The WHO's US office, the Pan American Health Organization, is in Washington, DC.

SOURCE
NOTES

CHAPTER 1. WATCHING WUHAN

1. "Coronavirus Death of Wuhan Doctor Sparks Anger." *BBC*, 7 Feb. 2020, bbc.com. Accessed 24 June 2020.

2. "Coronavirus Death of Wuhan Doctor Sparks Anger."

3. Erin Schumaker. "Mysterious Pneumonia Outbreak Sickens Dozens in China." *ABC News*, 6 Jan. 2020, abcnews.go.com. Accessed 24 June 2020.

4. "2009 H1N1 Pandemic (H1N1pdm09 virus)." *Centers for Disease Control and Prevention*, 11 June 2019, cdc.gov. Accessed 24 June 2020.

5. Lisa E. Gralinski and Vineet D. Menacherty. "Return of the Coronavirus: 2019-nCoV." *Viruses*, vol. 12, no. 2, 2020. 135.

CHAPTER 2. CORONAVIRUSES

1. "SARS Basic Fact Sheet." *Centers for Disease Control and Prevention*, n.d., cdc.gov. Accessed 24 June 2020.

2. Luis P. Villarreal. "Are Viruses Alive?" *Scientific American*, 8 Aug. 2008, scientificamerican.com. Accessed 13 Apr. 2020.

3. Jon Hamilton. "Doctors Link COVID-19 to Potentially Deadly Blood Clots and Strokes." *NPR*, 29 Apr. 2020, npr.org. Accessed 1 May 2020.

CHAPTER 3. THE SPREAD OF COVID-19

1. Jessica Murray et al. "Two People Die in Iran As Cruise Ship Britons Face Wirral Quarantine." *Guardian*, 19 Feb. 2020, theguardian.com. Accessed 24 June 2020.

2. Derrick Bryson Taylor. "A Timeline of the Coronavirus Pandemic." *New York Times*, 21 Apr. 2020, nytimes.com. Accessed 22 Apr. 2020.

3. Matteo Chinazzi, et al. "The Effect of Travel Restrictions on the Spread of the 2019 Novel Coronavirus (COVID-19) Outbreak." *Science*, vol. 369, no. 6489, 24 Apr. 2020. 395–400.

4. Helen Ward et al. "The Basic Reproduction Number." *Science Matters: Let's Talk about Covid-19, Imperial College London*, Coursera, 2020. coursera.org/learn/covid-19.

5. Jessica Migala. "How Is Coronavirus Spread?" *Health*, 3 Apr. 2020, health.com. Accessed 22 Apr. 2020.

6. Nicoletta Lanese. "Super-Spreader in South Korea Infects Nearly 40 People with Coronavirus." *Live Science*, 23 Feb. 2020, livescience.com. Accessed 22 Apr. 2020.

7. Elizabeth Williamson and Kristin Hussey. "How a Soiree in Connecticut Became a Super Spreader." *New York Times*, 23 Mar. 2020, nytimes.com. Accessed 22 Apr. 2020.

8. "Coronavirus in the U.S.: Latest Map and Case Count." *New York Times*, 22 Apr. 2020, nytimes.com. Accessed 22 Apr. 2020.

CHAPTER 4. PANDEMIC RESPONSES

1. Justin Fox. "How Bad Is the Coronavirus?" *Bloomberg*, 5 Mar. 2020, bloomberg.com. Accessed 25 June 2020.

2. "Ebola Virus Disease." *World Health Organization*, 21 June 2020, who.int. Accessed 24 June 2020.

3. "1918 Pandemic (H1N1 Virus)." *Centers for Disease Control and Prevention*, 20 Mar. 2019, cdc.gov. Accessed 24 June 2020.

4. Dan Barry and Caitlin Dickerson. "The Killer Flu of 1918: A Philadelphia Story." *New York Times*, 10 Apr. 2020, nytimes.com. Accessed 23 Apr. 2020.

5. Robert Belshe. "A Century of Influenza Prevention in St. Louis." *Missouri Medicine*, vol. 109, no. 2, 2012. 119–123.

6. Dan Goldberg. "Trump's Changing Tone on Coronavirus." *Politico*, 17. Mar. 2020, politico.com. Accessed 24 June 2020.

7. Grace Hauck et al. "Four Months In: A Timeline of How Covid-19 Unfolded in the US." *USA Today*, 20 May 2020, usatoday.com. Accessed 20 May 2020.

8. Hauck et al. "Four Months In."

9. Alberto Nardelli and Emily Ashton. "Everyone in Iceland Can Get Tested for the Coronavirus." *Buzzfeed News*, 18 Mar. 2020, buzzfeed.com. Accessed 7 Apr. 2020.

10. Alicia Lee. "What Is Herd Immunity and Why Some Think It Could End the Coronavirus Pandemic." *CNN*, 23 Apr. 2020, cnn.com. Accessed 23 Apr. 2020.

11. Morgan McFall-Johnsen. "Herd Immunity Is the Only Way the Coronavirus Pandemic Will End – And It Would Require a Vaccine. Here's How It Works." *Business Insider*, 14 Apr. 2020, businessinsider.com. Accessed 23 Apr. 2020.

12. "Sweden's Tegnell Admits Too Many Died." *BBC*, 3 June 2020. bbc.com. Accessed 1 July 2020.

13. McFall-Johnsen, "Herd Immunity Is the Only Way."

14. C. Jason Wang et al. "Response to Covid-19 in Taiwan." *JAMA*, vol. 323, no. 24, 2020.

CHAPTER 5. TESTING FOR COVID-19

1. Stefan Nicola. "A Berlin Biotech Company Has a Head Start on Coronavirus Tests." *Bloomberg Businessweek*, 12 Mar. 2020, bloomberg.com. Accessed 24 June 2020.

2. Nicola, "A Berlin Biotech Company Has a Head Start."

3. Sheri Fink and Mike Baker. "How Delays in Testing Set Back the U.S. Coronavirus Response." *New York Times*, 10 Mar. 2020, nytimes.com. Accessed 6 Apr. 2020.

4. Morgan McFall-Johnsen. "The CDC Has Broadened Its Coronavirus Testing Standards." *Business Insider*, 4 Mar. 2020, businessinsider.com. Accessed 24 Apr. 2020.

5. Aylin Woodward and Shayanne Gal. "One Chart Shows How Many Coronavirus Tests Per Capita Have Been Completed in 6 Countries." *Business Insider*, 20 Apr. 2020, businessinsider.com. Accessed 24 Apr. 2020.

6. Keith Collins. "Coronavirus Testing Needs to Triple Before the US Can Reopen, Experts Say." *New York Times*, 17 Apr. 2020, nytimes.com. Accessed 24 Apr. 2020.

7. Alberto Nardelli and Emily Ashton. "Everyone in Iceland Can Get Tested for the Coronavirus." *Buzzfeed News*, 18 Mar. 2020, buzzfeed.com. Accessed 7 Apr. 2020.

8. Nardelli and Ashton, "Everyone in Iceland Can Get Tested for the Coronavirus."

9. Nardelli and Ashton, "Everyone in Iceland Can Get Tested for the Coronavirus."

10. Nardelli and Ashton, "Everyone in Iceland Can Get Tested for the Coronavirus."

11. Robert P. Baird. "What Went Wrong with Coronavirus Testing in the U.S." *New Yorker*, 16 Mar. 2020, newyorker.com. Accessed 24 Apr. 2020.

12. Conor Hale. "Covid-19 Antibody Testing 'A Disaster,' Says Roche CEO, As Diagnostic Sales Rise." *FierceBiotech*, 22 Apr. 2020, fiercebiotech.com. Accessed 24 Apr. 2020.

SOURCE NOTES
CONTINUED

CHAPTER 6. TREATING COVID-19

1. "Hopes Dashed As Coronavirus Drug Remdesivir 'Fails First Trial.'" *BBC*, 23 Apr. 2020, bbc.com. Accessed 25 Apr. 2020.

2. "NIH Clinical Trial Shows Remdesivir Accelerates Recovery from Advanced COVID-19." *National Institutes of Health*, 29 Apr. 2020, nih.gov. Accessed 24 June 2020.

3. Adam Bienkov. "Scientists Fear the Hunt for a Coronavirus Vaccine Will Fail." *Business Insider*, 25 Apr. 2020, businessinsider.com. Accessed 25 Apr. 2020.

4. Eric Boodman. "Researchers Rush to Test Coronavirus Vaccine in People without First Knowing How Well It Works in Animals." *STAT*, 11 Mar. 2020, statnews.com. Accessed 24 June 2020.

5. Bienkov, "Scientists Fear the Hunt for a Coronavirus Vaccine Will Fail."

6. Bienkov, "Scientists Fear the Hunt for a Coronavirus Vaccine Will Fail."

7. Andrea Dukakis. "Doctors and Nurses Take on New Roles Amid Coronavirus." *CPR News*, 24 Apr. 2020, cpr.org. Accessed 21 May 2020.

8. Marlene Cimons. "SARS-CoV-2 Is Mutating Slowly, and That's a Good Thing." *Johns Hopkins University*, 10 June 2020, hub.jhu.edu. Accessed 24 June 2020.

9. Carl Zimmer. "Genes May Leave Some People More Vulnerable to COVID-19." *New York Times*, 3 June 2020, nytimes.com. Accessed 12 June 2020.

10. Miguel Marquez and Sonia Moghe. "Inside a Brooklyn Hospital That Is Overwhelmed with COVID-19 Patients and Deaths." *CNN*, 31 Mar. 2020, cnn.com. Accessed 20 May 2020.

11. "COVID-19: Data." *NYC Health*, n.d., nyc.gov. Accessed 1 June 2020.

12. Annie Reneau. "Dyson Designed a Coronavirus-Specific Ventilator in Just 10 Days." *Upworthy*, 29 Mar. 2020, upworthy.com. Accessed April 7, 2020.

CHAPTER 7. ECONOMIC IMPACT

1. Robert J. Shiller. "Predictions for the Coronavirus Stock Market." *New York Times*, 2 Apr. 2020, nytimes.com. Accessed 26 Apr. 2020.

2. "Oil Price Collapses to Lowest Level for 18 Years." *BBC*, 30 Mar. 2020, bbc.com. Accessed 26 Apr. 2020.

3. Danielle Wiener-Bronner. "Orange Juice Sales Are Soaring During the Pandemic." *CNN Business*, 9 Apr. 2020, cnn.com. Accessed 26 Apr. 2020.

4. Eric Martin. "Coronavirus Economic Impact Will Be Severe, at Least As Bad As Great Recession, Says IMF." *Fortune*, 13 Mar. 2020, fortune.com. Accessed 24 June 2020.

5. Jeff Cox. "A Record 20.5 Million Jobs Were Lost in April As Unemployment Rate Jumps to 14.7%." *CNBC*, 8 May 2020, cnbc.com. Accessed 24 June 2020.

6. Ella Koeze. "The $600 Unemployment Booster Shot, State by State." *New York Times*, 23 Apr. 2020, nytimes.com. Accessed 26 Apr. 2020.

7. Jennifer Liu. "New Relief Bill Boasts Unemployment Insurance by $600 a Week for Gig Workers, Freelancers, and More." *CNBC*, 2 Apr. 2020, cnbc.com. Accessed 26 Apr. 2020.

CHAPTER 8. RACIAL AND CULTURAL DISPARITIES

1. "2019 Novel Coronavirus Outbreak." *Washington State Department of Health*, n.d., doh.wa.gov. Accessed 23 May 2020.

2. "COVID-19 Statistics." *Illinois Department of Public Health*, n.d., dph.illinois.gov. Accessed 23 May 2020.

3. Cheyenne Haslett. "CDC Releases New Data As Debate Grows Over Racial Disparities in Coronavirus Deaths." *ABC News*, 8 Apr. 2020, abcnews.go.com. Accessed 26 Apr. 2020.

4. Haslett, "CDC Releases New Data."

5. Adam Cancryn. "Where Coronavirus Could Find a Refuge: Native American Reservations." *Politico*, 28 Mar. 2020, politico.com. Accessed 10 Apr. 2020.

6. Cancryn, "Where Coronavirus Could Find a Refuge."

7. Rachel Nania. "Blacks, Hispanics Hit Harder by the Coronavirus, Early U.S. Data Show." *AARP*, 9 Apr. 2020, aarp.org. Accessed 10 Apr. 2020.

8. Nania, "Blacks, Hispanics Hit Harder by the Coronavirus."

9. Nania, "Blacks, Hispanics Hit Harder by the Coronavirus."

10. Haslett, "CDC Releases New Data."

11. Haslett, "CDC Releases New Data."

12. Rachel Sugar. "The Scramble to Feed the Kids Left Hungry by the Coronavirus Crisis." *Vox*, 17 Apr. 2020, vox.com. Accessed 26 Apr. 2020.

13. Tahla Burki. "Prisons Are in 'No Way Equipped' to Deal with COVID-19." *Lancet*. 2 May 2020, thelancet.com. Accessed 23 May 2020.

14. Katie Park et al. "Tracking the Spread of Coronavirus in Prisons." *Marshall Project*, 24 Apr. 2020, themarshallproject.org. Accessed 23 May 2020.

15. Gaby Galvin. "Language Access Issues a Barrier During COVID-19." *US News and World Report*, 16 Apr. 2020, usnews.com. Accessed 26 Apr. 2020.

16. Janell Ross. "Coronavirus Outbreak Revives Dangerous Race Myths and Pseudoscience." *NBC News*, 19 Mar. 2020, nbcnews.com. Accessed 26 Apr. 2020.

17. Aleem Maqbool. "Coronavirus: Why Has the Virus Hit African Americans So Hard?" *BBC*, 11 Apr. 2020, nbcnews.com. Accessed 26 Apr. 2020.

18. Nania, "Blacks, Hispanics Hit Harder by the Coronavirus."

CHAPTER 9. THE FUTURE

1. David A. Graham. "Why Are the States Reopening?" *Atlantic*, 23 May 2020, theatlantic.com. Accessed 12 June 2020.

2. Marlene Cimons. "SARS-CoV-2 Is Mutating Slowly, and That's a Good Thing." *Johns Hopkins University*, 10 June 2020, hub.jhu.edu. Accessed 24 June 2020.

3. Graham, "Why Are the States Reopening?"

4. "South Korea Closes Schools Again after Biggest Spike in Weeks." *BBC*, 29 May 2020, bbc.com. Accessed 12 June 2020.

5. Robert Langreth and Susan Berfield. "Famed AIDS Researcher Is Racing to Find a Coronavirus Treatment." *Bloomberg Businessweek*, 19 Mar. 2020, bloomberg.com. Accessed 24 June 2020.

6. Langreth and Berfield, "Famed AIDS Researcher."

7. "Outbreak Brief 19: COVID-19 Pandemic – 26 May 2020." *Africa CDC*, 26 May 2020, africacdc.org. Accessed 24 June 2020.

8. Nicholas Bariyo and Joe Parkinson. "Coronavirus Might Become 'Fixture' in Africa for Years." *Wall Street Journal*, 23 May 2020, wsj.com. Accessed 24 June 2020.

INDEX

acquired immunodeficiency syndrome
(AIDS), 13–14, 63, 65
antibodies, 11, 46, 52, 58–59, 62,
65–67, 70
antivirals, 62–64
leronlimab, 63
remdesivir, 63–64

basic reproduction numbers (R0),
32–33, 96
bats, 7, 19, 98
blood clots, 23
Brazil, 26, 62
Bush, George W., 43

Chicago, Illinois, 37
Chu, Helen, 33–37
clinics, 4, 15, 31, 53
colds, 4, 20, 57
community liaisons, 91
Coronavirus Aid, Relief, and Economic
Security (CARES) Act, 80–81
coughing, 7, 15, 20–21, 30–32, 33,
43, 60
curve, the, 48–49

doctors, 4–7, 15, 23, 33–36, 46, 47,
49, 53–54, 60, 62, 70, 71, 72,
74, 84

Ebola, 40, 63, 66, 98
Elba, Idris, 90

face masks, 15, 32, 48, 53, 60, 92
Fauci, Anthony, 84
fevers, 7, 9, 15, 20–21, 30, 34, 40,
47, 60
Food and Drug Administration (FDA),
US, 54, 64, 73
France, 26, 53

GenBank, 13
Germany, 14, 50

hand sanitizer, 24
herd immunity, 45–47, 96
Ho, David, 13–14, 65, 98
Huanan Seafood Wholesale Market,
4, 7, 9, 10, 31
Hubei province, China, 7, 15

Iceland, 55–57
Italy, 26, 45, 55, 56, 62, 71, 72

Japan, 26, 64
Johns Hopkins University, 44, 70,
94
Johnson, Boris, 47

Landt, Olfert, 14, 50, 51
Li Wenliang, 6, 7
Lyme disease, 10

Middle East respiratory syndrome
  (MERS), 9, 20, 98

New York City, 37, 55, 62, 63, 65,
  71, 87
Newsom, Gavin, 44
1918 flu pandemic, 40–41
nurses, 49

Obama, Barack, 43
oil prices, 78

Philadelphia, Pennsylvania, 41
Philippines, the, 26
pneumonia, 4–7, 9, 62
prisons, 88

quarantine, 4, 38, 40, 45, 48

recession, 76–78, 80, 81

Saint Louis, Missouri, 40–42
Saudi Arabia, 20–21
severe acute respiratory syndrome
  (SARS), 6, 9, 20, 38–40, 50, 98
Snohomish County, Washington
  State, 15, 30, 35
social distancing, 31–32, 38, 40–45,
  47–48, 56, 69, 79, 89–90, 92,
  96
sore throats, 9, 21
South Korea, 20–21, 26, 34, 53, 55,
  56, 64, 95–96

steroids, 64
stock prices, 77–78
super spreaders, 34
Sweden, 46–47
swine flu pandemic (2009 H1N1
  influenza), 11, 50

Taiwan, 12, 48
temporary hospitals, 62
testing for COVID-19, 23, 31, 34,
  35–37, 45, 50–57, 58–59, 87
Thailand, 26
travel bans, 28–31
Trump, Donald, 43–44, 67–68,
  94–95, 98

unemployment, 79–80, 81, 87, 94
United Kingdom, the, 24, 47, 64,
  69, 78
University of California, Irvine, 20, 21

vaccines, 13, 23, 46, 62, 66–71,
  94, 99
ventilators, 22, 62–63, 69, 71,
  72–73

Waka Flocka Flame, 90
Wei Guixian, 4
Whitty, Christopher, 69
Wilson, Jenny, 91
World Health Organization (WHO), 6,
  9, 31, 50, 98
Wuhan, China, 4–7, 10, 12–13, 15, 21,
  26, 28–29, 31, 33, 37, 55, 98, 99

ABOUT THE
AUTHOR

SUE BRADFORD EDWARDS

Sue Bradford Edwards is a Missouri nonfiction author who writes about society and history. She is the author or coauthor of 20 other titles from Abdo Publishing, including *The Murders of Tupac and Biggie*, *The Assassination of John F. Kennedy*, and *Hidden Human Computers*. She socially isolated at home during the COVID-19 pandemic with her husband and son, writing books for young readers, reading, and watching Star Wars and Harry Potter movies.